Dating
Confidential

a singles guide to a fun, flirtatious
and possibly meaningful social life

Hedda Muskat

SOURCEBOOKS CASABLANCA™
AN IMPRINT OF SOURCEBOOKS, INC.®
NAPERVILLE, ILLINOIS

Published by Sourcebooks, Inc.

P.O. Box 4410, Naperville, Illinois 60567-4410

(630) 961-3900

FAX: (630) 961-2168

www.sourcebooks.com

ISBN 1-4022-0201-6

Library of Congress Cataloging-in-Publication Data

Muskat, Hedda.

Dating confidential : a singles guide to a fun, flirtatious and possibly meaningful social life / by Hedda Muskat.

p. cm.

ISBN 1-4022-0201-6 (alk. paper)

1. Dating (Social customs) I. Title.

HQ801.M87 2004

646.7'7—dc22

2004005152

Printed and bound in the United States of America

ED   10   9   8   7   6   5   4   3   2   1

To my precious daughter Lindsay

Special thanks to the hundreds of singles
who revealed their feelings to me
with honesty, courage, and sincerity.

Table of Contents

chapter one

Why You Should Read This Book

According to www.itsjustlunch.com, there are one hundred million singles in the U.S.! That's a lot of single men and women. If you're single, this book is for you. Especially if you've been wondering lately...

Is there someone out there for you?

Yes!!! There is definitely someone out there for you.

If you follow all these dating tips, you will be guaranteed to have a date this weekend. With one hundred million singles out there, you don't need to sit home alone with your buddy, Häagen-Dazs, unless that's your choice.

The true secret behind successful dating is taking the ball in your hand and making it happen. I don't mean to make it sound easy, because it's not. I know what it's like to have a close relationship with Häagen-Dazs, and all its relatives. I know what it's like to be rejected. I also know what it's like to do a makeover on my life, lose those few extra pounds, get a new haircut and new jeans, and start meeting people. As comforting as it is to pick up the phone and order that pizza at midnight, it's more comforting to have someone to share it with.

So put that spoon down, take a shower, put on something that makes you feel sexy, call a friend, and go out.

This part is really that easy. It's the rest of it where the "games" begin!

WHY THIS BOOK APPLIES TO YOU

If you're single and fit into one of the categories below, you may feel you're playing a different dating game than the rest of us. Well, how's it going? If you're even the least bit dissatisfied, then this book is a must-read for you, too.

Gorgeous Model-Type Girls

It seems to be a belief in our society that there are gorgeous women who effortlessly get all the men they want. However, the reason they still need all the dating advice they can get is because being truly gorgeous is a fantasy.

Ever look at a model without her make up? It's quite scary. Eventually, the looks start fading, their power diminishes, and they need the same tools as the rest of us.

That's why average-looking women do much better in the long run, because their mates grow to love them based on *who* they are, not based on how skinny they are.

Ever hear a man say "I love my wife more now than I did when I married her"? Okay, not all men say that, but learn from the ones who do. It's aimed at those women who truly take care of themselves as they grow older, and take care of their man. A woman who takes care of her man by being his friend and lover will get a lot more back from him as well. If she doesn't get anything back from him, then that's a deeper problem and a different book.

Rich Men

There seems to be another misconception that, no matter how attractive or unattractive a man is, if he's got money, he can get almost any woman he wants. This *may* hold true at the beginning of the relationship.

While the girl you're with is out having a good time with your credit cards, if you don't do all the other little things that count in life for her, then don't be surprised if she brings home something more from the mall than just another pair of $400 shoes. Another guy may show her love like she's never seen.

But why even talk about long-term relationships, when this is a book about dating?

Because in order to get to the light at the end of the tunnel, you need to get past the first date.

Everyone wants someone with whom to share his or her life. *Dating Confidential* is going to show you how to get there.

THE REAL SECRET BEHIND DATING

Making Choices. That's really it. Two words. Making choices. If you continually repeat this, almost as a chant, the mystery of the dating world will all unravel.

Successful dating is about all sorts of choices:

- The choice to date at all
- The choice to better yourself
- The choice to have sex
- The choice to make the call

- The choice to say yes
- The choice to remain single

BUT WHY LISTEN TO ME?

I'm not a psychologist, sociologist, or any other "ologist."

I'm not some preacher on the radio telling you that you're a total loser if you're single. For some, single is just fine.

I'm not some angry bitch who needs a book to let out all her steam as to why men suck. Men are actually great. I'm tired of hearing women complain that all men are dogs. I happen to love dogs. You just need to find the right dog for you.

Women are great. I'm tired of hearing men call all women gold diggers and bitches. This is the kind of woman a man *chooses* to date. You can't change her from wanting material things from you or being the bitch she is. You can only change the choice to date her. *Back to choices.*

So, who am I?

I'm a writer who worked on TV's most successful and longest running dating show, *Love Connection with Chuck Woolery*. I interviewed over six hundred singles to find out what turned them on and off about their dates. Guys told me intimate things about what really got them excited about a woman, and things that made them want to run.

The ladies shared with me details about how even good-looking men can lose if they do stupid things. This book shares all those secret, intimate details about what really turns people on and off.

I also spoke to my friends—single people of all ages. The ones who took my advice are truly having a great dating life. One friend is now dating a lawyer that she met in the supermarket. She's also on a diet and plans to give herself a complete makeover, after having three kids in ten years. She's living her life with a new look, and a new man. She made the choice. The ones who closed their ears to any advice from anyone are still single and dateless. But that's okay too. Because another big secret in having a successful dating life is to *want to date*. They weren't ready. They said they were waiting for this book to come out.

I was also single. I was never the one who men jumped through hoops to meet at a party because looking back, I didn't dress to my potential. I hid my body, hid my sex appeal, in fear that I would have to come through in the end. It was easier to be the one in the corner. In my mid thirties, when I realized that I was missing out, I made the choice to lose some weight, buy some sexy clothes, and get out there. Wow! What a difference that made. I was getting calls, dates, and I had choices. However, although my look changed, I was still the insecure, sexually shy person on the inside. I still had to work on that. *That was another choice to make.*

So if dating is just all about choices...why do we continuously make the wrong ones?

By the end of this book you'll see why.

What You Won't Hear From This Book

1. **I don't want to tell you things that will annoy you, like "trust your intuition."** This feeling flies out the window as fear, insecurities, and doubt set in.

2. **I don't want to tell you there are dating rules.** Rules such as: *don't leave your toothbrush at your date's house*, or *no sex on the first date*. The reality, based on all my interviews, is that *there are no dating rules*.

After you read this book, you will continue to use it as your handy-dandy guide just before you go out. You'll need it in times of awkward silent moments.

Dating Confidential is your friend. What's great about having a book as your friend is that you don't have to feed it, walk it, or talk to it. It's here to guide you and for you to rely on when no one else is around.

SEXISM AND DATING

How far have we come since our parents or grandparents dated in the '50s?

Although technology has changed, the dating scene is still filled with anxiety, uncertainty, and fear. This will never change. Other than women making their own way, and having more power, and wearing pants, nothing has changed with regard to how men really relate to women.

Two Hard Facts About Men and Women

1 Men are not drawn to a woman's brain at first.

2 Women are drawn to the size of a man's pocket and what's in it at first.

Both true. This may sound shallow, offensive, degrading, and insulting, but after interviewing over six hundred singles, these were the two facts that stood out the most.

Going into dating knowing these two facts is the reason why this book is going to be your best dating guide ever. It stays focused on the realities of dating life. I'm here to present to you the facts as they were presented to me.

SEX APPEAL

So naturally, the first question is, what makes a woman sexy?

Her Body

Does she have to look like a Victoria's Secret model, or have a stick figure like Cameron Diaz? What message is Christina Aguilera sending us by packing on twenty pounds to look more curvaceous?

According to the men between the ages of twenty and sixty that I spoke to, men love women who have curves, but not flab. They love a woman who walks tall, and has nice-fitting clothes. It's not the stick-thin woman that they love, but rather the woman who has the curves in the right places.

This is good news for women who are on a perpetual diet. The message here is: *Don't be skinny, but bulge doesn't work either*. Wear flattering clothes that show off butt and cleavage. Once again, this may sound shallow, insulting, or degrading, but it is true.

Her Hair

Men also love shiny, long to medium cut hair. So if you've got razor blade short hair, you may want to grow it out. Men love hair they can run their fingers through. Tight braids, hair spray, or hair extensions are not sexy to a man. Clean, simple hair. That's what he likes.

Her Attitude

Men love women who look like they know "they've got it going on." That means they feel sexy, and walk the walk. Ladies, the next time you're in a mall, observe how men look and react to different women. The woman who walks with grace and style gets more attention then the woman who slouches over, and is hiding her body under layers of clothes.

Women should try this experiment on their own. Go to the same place at two different times wearing two different styles of clothing. Take a friend with a video camera and see for yourself the kind of looks you'll get from men. It's worth the time and effort.

What Makes a Man Sexy?

For a first impression, it's his profession and his income.

Women love men who have it together. No matter how successful a woman is in her profession, statistically, women still have it harder on the work front. It truly is still a man's world. A man can get away with a lot more incompetence at work, whereas a woman always has to prove herself.

Women are attracted to a man who has the potential to give her the choice to work or to not work. Being with a man who offers no financial stability is a turn-off. It limits her choices. It limits her future. Why waste time with a poor guy if you can get a guy who has some money? Yes, it's shallow, offensive, degrading, and insulting, *but true.* At least for the first date. Getting beyond dating and into a relationship is going to call for more from a man, but at the beginning, women equate financial security with the emotional security they're ultimately seeking.

Look no further than Prince Charles. Take away his income, palace, jewels, and throne...throw him in a Postal Worker's uniform, driving a Pinto to his mobile home in Montana, and what have you got?

Yes, this too is shallow, offensive, degrading, and insulting, *but true.*

DATING SECRETS FROM THE
LOVE CONNECTION COUCH

Having had the privilege of working on television's longest-running syndicated dating show, *Love Connection*, I learned first hand what really went on with the couples you saw on TV. As the writer on the show, I had to interview the couples right after their date, and write up the story for the show.

I interviewed hundreds of people—men, women, young, old, widowed, divorced, and scorned. I met them all and heard it all. What you saw on the show was real. If a woman said her first impression of her date was that he looked like the *Pillsbury Doughboy,* that was *real*. We didn't write those lines. We only wrote the facts of the story.

If the man said her ass was *"bigger than an elephant's,"* that was real, too. I wrote up the facts and presented the story to Chuck, highlighting the funny, sad, insulting moments.

I told the contestants only to dwell on the insulting parts. That's what made the show great. The insults and Chuck's looks were the real secret behind the success of the show. Was that mean of me to do? How could I look at myself in the mirror when decent people left our studio emotionally bruised?

It was simple. They came to us. They wanted to be on TV and took the risk. The good dates were boring. The bad dates were exciting. Why the *bad* dates? Because for the most part, those were the dates we could relate to. We've all been there. Sad but true. We saw ourselves.

Since I am still working as a writer, and now producer, in television and in reality programming, I can tell you first hand that all these new dating TV shows have people scared and mixed up about dating and dating expectations. The reality dating shows of today are not really what happens. The contestants you see are recruited from "wanna be" acting agencies and will do and say anything to get on TV. Those people are prepped and coached by the producers on what to say and how to act.

Love Connection was real. We used real people and really wrote up what happened on the dates. Yes, I'm not going to hide the fact that these people were coached, but they were coached to say the highlights of what really happened on the date.

I'm not knocking those crazy reality shows on TV, either. They are fun, entertaining, and provide an escape from the real world. All I'm saying is that you don't want to treat them as if this is really what's going on.

SO WHY AM I TALKING ABOUT MY *LOVE CONNECTION* SECRETS NOW?

I'd been banking these stories for years, thinking that one day I'd share these steamy secrets with you. But then I looked on Amazon.com, plugged in "dating," and saw close to two thousand books come up. So I thought, "Is there a need for another dating book?"

While I found most of the books on dating to be written in an easy-to-read fashion (because I like small words, little chapters, and words that get to the point—even if they have no relevance), the problem with many of these books is that the hype of the book makes more sense than the book. They just don't work. Although I'm sure the authors have done well financially with their books, for the most part I feel books like this will mix people up and create more confusion.

So, with two thousand dating books out there, some did contain useful tips, but you had to plod through mountains of extraneous stuff just to get to the meat.

I felt it was time to dust off all my *Love Connection* notes, get back into the field, and start talking to singles again. I wanted to write a book that would eliminate the need for two thousand dating books. If you need that many, something's not right. I'm here to change that. *That's the choice I have made!*

I continued to read those dating books to see what *not* to do. I don't want to pack this book with dating disaster stories, dating anecdotes, and dating analysis. Just get to the point.

Dating Confidential is the *meat*. No side dishes. No dessert. No psycho jargon, no analysis, no what happened to you as a child, and why your mother's to blame for your boring messed up single life. *Dating Confidential* is *just* the meat. What men and women really need to know to get past the first date.

Love Connection did make "real" connections for some. Out of the thousands of couples that dated over the eleven years the show was on the air, some really made it.

Dating Confidential will share with you proven methods of what worked and what didn't.

Dating Confidential is your own personal dating checklist.

Use these bullet points as a reminder of all the things you should be doing before you go out. This is will give you the confidence you need to get through the scariness of the first date. You may not feel 100 percent comfortable, but I guarantee that you will feel pretty close.

Don't be too shy to give this to friends or to bring it on your date. This guide makes for great conversation. You're not the only one reading these books. With the thousands of advice books on the market, someone is reading them. This is the only guide that really holds you by the hand...step by step. You can spend hours in therapy, hours talking your friend's ear off, but if you truly understand the concepts in this guide, it will come together for you.

Dating Confidential is here to tell you:

- How to get ready
- What to do
- How to meet
- What to say
- How to look
- How to get intimate

OVERCOMING FEARS

Dating is a packed word. It drums up images of a nerve-wracking time, filled with doubts and unfulfilled expectations.

- Am I attractive enough?
- Am I saying stupid things?
- Do I have bad breath?
- Is something stuck in my teeth?
- How do I handle the first kiss?
- What happens after that?

All these fears can really mess up your date, and may even make you behave in a way that's not really you. Anxiety, stress, and panic have turned people off from traditional dating. Some say turbulence on an Alaskan Airlines MD80 flying over the ocean is less stressful than going out on a date.

So why all this panic over dating? Was it this hard for our parents? Probably not. That's because the roles of men and women were clearly defined. Men were the breadwinners, and the women stayed at home. Today, more men are working from home, and women are CEOs of major corporations.

Dating styles now will, by necessity, have a different approach and different outcomes. Lots of people have lost their life savings in the crashing stock market, have lost jobs, and don't have their parents to financially save them anymore. Yuppies and baby boomers who were hoping for that nice inheritance are finding themselves "cash poor." That's why things like Internet dating, speed dating, and lunch dates have been so successful. It takes away many of the old traditional dating rituals, such as going out to an expensive dinner, show, dancing, and drinks. It takes away the risk of spending a lot of your hard-earned money on someone you don't really care about.

It also takes away some of the romance, but that's okay, because you can make it up on the second date. You can still be romantic at Starbucks. Women love men who can be romantic anywhere. A man doesn't need to spend a lot of money to wow a woman on their first date. He just needs to make her feel like she's the only one in the room. Even if it is over a frappuchino.

DATING TRENDS

Hard work, smart investing, and more exotic dating is the way people are going. By exotic I mean not relying on traditional set ups or the bar scene to find a date. This generation of daters is more conservative in investing and really does want to retire young. What they lack in daring in their financial endeavors, they make up for in their personal lives. They are far more experimental and daring in the dating world than our parents ever were. They want instant gratification. They want to find it with the least amount of work. They want it now. It's as easy as switching on your computer and logging on somewhere. You can have five dates planned for the weekend without ever getting out of your pajamas.

People who really don't want to waste any time can meet on line and plan an instant weekend getaway. For some, that works. The point is that, as cautious as we now are with how we spend our money, we want to be more adventurous and take more risks in our social life.

However, as creative and different as these new approaches to dating may be, successful dating will always be based on the reality of...

What really turns a man on, and what really turns a woman on.

MEN ARE VISUAL...
AND WOMEN ARE EMOTIONAL

You can't change that. No matter how much you spend on the date, no matter how creative you are in planning the date, no matter how much fun you have, the bottom line is that the man has to be physically attracted to the woman, and for the woman to be attracted to a man, he has to appeal to her emotions.

This is all you have to know. You can't change the man, you can't change the woman. It's a genetic make-up that's there. If you can keep this in the back of your mind when you go out, and you find you don't get the call back or the first kiss, then *he/she wasn't into you.* That's it. Period. Move on; maybe the next one will be.

However, keep in mind that lust can cloud your judgment. You can lust for someone, but it doesn't mean he or she is right for you. This book isn't about *lust*, but it's still important to be honest with yourself and recognize the difference. We all have been there...where lust has taken us down a dangerous path. Lust can be fun, sexy, and as thrilling as going on a roller coaster, breaking all sound barriers. But it can also be sabotaging, turning you into a possessive, insecure, desperate, and pathetic person. Remember, a relationship solely based on lust is something everyone has experienced and you haven't lived until you've been through this.

WHY PEOPLE FEAR DATING SO MUCH

Rejection is the biggest reason why singles hate the dating scene. No one is programmed emotionally to really deal with it. But now I'm going to tell you the best way of dealing with rejection.

First of all, it's human nature to want to crawl back into your igloo when it comes to rejection. No human being enjoys it. Whether it's rejection from a date, or rejection from a job—any kind—it doesn't feel good.

So you must find healthy ways to deal with it. Find the things that *do* make you feel good about yourself. Surround yourself with people who, when you walk away from them, don't make you feel worse about yourself. The worst thing you can do is have a group of friends or family members that reminds you of your flaws. Unless these are flaws you can change, or that make sense to you, keep a distance from them. You don't want to be reminded that you're too stupid to earn more than minimum wage, or that you've got a wide ass. There are people out there for you who will appreciate the fact that you even have a job. Minimum wage is better than no "wage" because it's a steady income, you can probably move up the ladder, and there are usually health benefits.

As far as the wide ass goes, there are men who love this. If you show confidence in yourself, your sex appeal will shine through.

If you're the type of person who can get over rejection quickly, that's great. If not, you may want to rely on friends, relatives, and co-workers to get you through the first part of helping you meet someone. A set up guarantees a date. It doesn't mean you'll have a second one, but at least you're going out!

If you are constantly being rejected, then it could be you. Use this book as your checklist to see if you can figure out why you think you're being rejected. But don't obsess over it. People have a hard time being honest about why they don't want to continue going out with a person and will find a safe excuse, which is usually the "it's not you, it's me" excuse. If you buy it fine, if not, go back through the date and think about what it could be. Most of the time, it's the whole chemistry thing, but that means you're going after the wrong type. You need to re-evaluate your choices. Again...choices. It's all about the choices we make.

If he doesn't call, or she doesn't respond to you, it's in your power to decide how you want to handle it. You can either keep blaming yourself, or move on. Please move on!!!! It's healthier.

But you also can't deny a natural response when you think the other person is into you and you get the blow off. There are many reasons for the blow off.

- no chemistry
- not ready to date, getting over bad break up
- the other person may be looking for things that you can't give him or her
- he or she is still in the closet
- you may have done something

It's not easy re-gaining your self-esteem after having your ego crushed. That's part of the risk. But with all risk can come great pleasure.

Keep your head focused…if it doesn't work out, move on. Don't stalk, don't sulk, and don't beat yourself up. Don't *ever* let another person have that power over you. Ever!!!! It's a choice you need to make.

WHAT HAPPENED ON THE
LOVE CONNECTION COUCH

Couples were split. One sat on the couch with Chuck, and the other was on a chair backstage with a camera that we could see onstage in a monitor.

When the couples arrived at the studio, we had them

park in different parking lots, as one of the rules to be on the show was that there was to be no contact before the taping of the show or after their date. The couples would be disqualified from the show if they saw each other again. The time from the date to the taping of the show was about two weeks, so you knew for those who had a *good* date, it was hard for them to stay apart.

This rule was based on trust, and by us calling them every day to probe to see if this rule had been broken. It was easy to crack. We had a knack for cornering them on the phone, the way a lawyer does during a deposition.

The person who did the selecting was given $75 for the date. I know that's not a lot, but the logic behind this was to see how creative the date would be. It also sparked great fights after, because if the person didn't spring for more cash out of pocket, you know he or she was going to be called cheap.

WHAT REALLY HAPPENED ON THE DATES?

Okay, here's the behind-the-scenes lowdown on what couples actually did on their first date.

Sex, Sex, and Lots of It.

There was a lot of drinking on these dates and as a result many had sex. If they didn't click after that, which most didn't because the sex was alcohol-related, it made for great TV. The women were embarrassed, and the guys felt pressured.

Very few of these ladies felt good about themselves the next day. The humiliation of sleeping with a guy who boots you out of his bed afterwards and puts you in a cab made women feel like chewed up and spit out meat.

I would ask the guys why they tossed these ladies out. The response was very honest. "I was horny, drunk, and wanted sex." So was that all it took to get a girl to have sex with him...getting her drunk? Yes.

How Much Drinking Was Really Involved?

Lots. The whole dating scene is filled with "getting drunk." Before dinner drinks, during dinner wine, then nightcaps. So if drinking and sex are so related, and the feelings the next day are those of humiliation and disgust...WHY DO IT?

FEAR!!!! Fear seems to be the constant with most daters. Alcohol took away all inhibitions, all worries, all fears...*and all self respect*. While you're sober, or partly sober, you still have the ability to make wise choices. You still have fear in you. Getting drunk takes away the fear factor, and it's easy to hop into bed.

So many girls would cry to me on the phone, saying, "How stupid could I have been? I really thought he loved me. We were planning a weekend getaway. He was going to take me to his cousin's wedding. I invited him for Easter brunch." All this from a first date? Ladies, please don't ever believe what a guy tells you during his horny getting-you-in-the-sack phase. See what he says to you as he's calling a cab. That's his truth. That should be yours, too.

I'm not saying don't drink. I love to drink. But I also try to know my limits. If drinking makes you become something you're not, don't do it. Don't blame the guy. A guy is a guy, and will do anything to get you to take your clothes off and have sex with him. He may even use the "love" word, which is really a cover up for another four-letter word!

Don't allow loneliness, desperation, or your biological clock to cloud your judgment. It's really not worth it.

During the tapings of the show, even when the date had been good, guys were flirting with our cute production assistants, giving them their numbers, while their dates thought they were going to have a second date. Just because a man has a good date with you it doesn't mean he won't date others. You should too.

THE TOP THREE THINGS THAT COUPLES SAY ABOUT THEIR DATES

Men Need to Be Physically Attracted to the Woman

"She's real nice. We could be friends."

"Her butt was so big it could stop a Mack truck."

"Aren't *Flashdance* fashions out of style?"

"She had a great body, but a horse's face."

"She had a great face, but a horse's ass."

Does this make men shallow, stupid pigs? No!!!

Men are *visual* and need to be visually stimulated. It's not their fault. They are born that way...so ladies need to get with the program.

They can't help it if they are shallow when it comes to their personal life. It's in their genetic make-up, and if they are honest enough, they will admit to it.

Women need to understand that men are simple. They don't like to talk too much unless they want to, unless it's about themselves, or unless it's about sex.

So never ask a man "what are you feeling?" He'll run the other way.

A man likes to discuss what he feels when he wants to. It's usually out of the blue, out of left field. It is also usually days after an incident happens. Men tend to keep things that bother them locked up and spring it on the woman when she least expects it, like after sex.

But women can use this to their advantage. In order for a man to be attracted to her, she doesn't have to take the car for a wash, be rich, wear socks that match, have polished shoes, or make great conversation.

All she has to do is look good. All women have this ability. Even the most unattractive ones!

Women Want Men to Have Money

Women would tell me that even though they were attracted to the guy, and had a great date, the big thing stopping them from proceeding was the fact that the guy had no money. The biggest turn-off for the woman was the man's income. However, if he worked at McDonald's, that would be okay...as long as he was the manager! Women like men who make the best of their jobs, show ambition, and have enough pocket change to pay for coffee afterwards.

Women don't want to hear men say this:

"I'm still working at 7-11, but I really want to be an actor."

"What do you mean, you never use public transportation?"

"Do you have money for the meter?"

"I picked these out of your neighbor's garden."

"Can we go Dutch?"

Does this make a woman a whore? No!!!

Women need to feel safe and secure. A man who has no money, or little stability, can't give her that. A woman's earning power is still much less than a man's. Even if she's an attorney, you'll find male lawyers with less talent earning more.

There are also women who will overlook a man's empty bank account if he:

- is in law school
- is in med school
- is starting a great business
- has family money
- just had his face in the paper as the state's newest ninety million lotto winner

There has to be a potential for money.

Once again, as much as men may call these women "gold diggers," for the most part, all a woman really wants is security. A man with any smarts will be able to tell the difference between the woman who is scared off by his lack of earning power and the woman who takes him shopping for diamonds on the first date.

Women Blab Too Much on the First Date

Men's biggest complaint was that from the moment he handed her the single rose, the next four hours were non-stop talk, talk, talk...

Men would tell me that their biggest turn-off would be how fast a woman would start yapping about her dream house, and how many children she wants before he had the chance to turn the car on. She would tell him how to drive, why he shouldn't eat meat, why he should work out more, and why he should dump all his college friends.

Are women really this controlling, opinionated, and annoying? Not really. It's a nervous mechanism that goes off when they don't know what else to say.

So how does the guy know this? He's not a mind reader. Most men wouldn't know this. That could be why there is no second date.

So How Did the Date End?

If she was pretty enough, all he wanted to do was get her drunk, get laid, and meet his friends for beers afterwards.

This was such a common story.

So what does it take to get to the second date and beyond? Read on...

chapter two:

Getting What You Want Out of Dating

WHAT DO YOU REALLY WANT?

Dating is a social way to meet a potential mate. Boy, does this sound simple. If it were this simple, there wouldn't be thousands of dating books, dating advice columnists, and call-in radio shows. We would all go out and live happily ever after.

Here's one simple answer!

We all have different reasons for dating, so if you're not in sync with the other person, it won't work.

How many times have you heard...

"I like you, but I just got over a bad break up and I'm not ready to settle down."

"I like you, but I'm not attracted to you."

"I like you, but I'm worried that your low-paying job won't get me the things I want in life."

"I like you, but I don't want to get involved with a bi-sexual."

There are hundreds of reasons why there is no second date.

One More Simple Answer That Can Change All This!!!

Chemistry. You can't make it, you can't explain it. It's just there. All the reasons why people date—or don't date—can go right out the window if there is no spark or tingling sensation. If the chemistry strikes, you're on your way. The problem with this is that for some, the chemistry is one-sided. That also won't work. For some, chemistry is really lust. That can work, if there really was chemistry and it's two-sided.

Sustaining the Chemistry

So you had great chemistry and now you're going out again. You start learning more things about each other. As the red flags come up, the chemistry part dies down a bit. By the end of the date, if there are more red flags than you want to handle, the chemistry part is over. It doesn't mean the guy still won't want to have sex with you. That's where lust comes in. Once again, it's hard to see if a guy is into you because of sincere chemistry or horny lust.

What is initial chemistry?

Initial chemistry is based on a visual reaction. It's based on just a look, and superficial dialogue. As you both open your mouths to talk that fantasy that you had about that person can either grow into something positive or die out.

That's why you hear people say, "I don't know what happened. We had so much chemistry at the beginning." That's right, baby. At the beginning. Now reality kicks in. Now the nagging starts. Now she starts telling him to skip golf with his friends and take her shopping instead. He tells her to give up yoga, pilates, or med school. This is when chemistry comes to a dead halt. This is why we have thousands of dating books and advice experts. This is why dating is more than chemistry. However, without the initial chemistry, it is very hard to get to the second date. No matter what you want out of the date, if there is no initial chemistry, consider it a friendship and not a date.

At *Love Connection,* I heard over and over how two people went out and had a great time, but wouldn't want to try a second date. The reason? No chemistry. They would then say, "but I see myself being friends with that person," or "I'd fuck her, but I wouldn't want to date her."

There is no such thing as a friendship date. It's either a friendship, or a date. It's very hard for women to have male friends who don't think about having sex with them. Unless they are gay, they really do want to have sex. That's the male make up. It won't change.

Don't equate a man who wants to have sex with you with having chemistry with you. *Men will still have sex with a woman, even if there is no chemistry. It's just sex. He doesn't even care if he knows her name.*

A man who has sex with a woman he has chemistry with will want to get to know her better. He'll insist on wanting to know her name. He'll want to take her out. A date based only on sex and lust usually won't entail an outing...unless it's in the back seat of the car.

SO WHY DATE?
Are You Dating Because You Just Want to Have Sex?

Nothing is wrong with this as long as you don't act like a jerk and mislead the other person. This is just common courtesy and decency, which this book won't teach you.

I have a very good friend, who is a single, successful, rich, gorgeous lawyer in his mid-thirties. He has no intentions of settling down until his mid-forties, when he is ready to slow down at work and have kids. He makes this clear with the women he meets. If he brings a woman home, he tells her that just because they are having sex, it doesn't mean there will be a second date. He also makes it clear that it also doesn't mean she's staying the whole night.

If a woman who wants to have a steady boyfriend meets this kind of guy, she must understand the consequences of having sex right away. Sleeping with you, no matter how great you are in the sack, won't make a person change. It may only make them want a second night in the sack. You can't change people, their goals, or their motives. However, what can change is the chemistry. If there is a mutual connection, then it is possible that what first started out as a one-night stand could blossom into a long-term relationship. That's the risk you take. Know it. Then you'll be able to look at yourself in the mirror.

Are You Dating for the Companionship and Because You Want a Relationship?

If this is what you're looking for, then why date the guy who takes you to his studio love shack without getting to know your name? The guy who has Polaroid pictures of his conquests all over his chipped, unpainted stucco wall. You know the guy. We all know the guy.

The guy with:

- wrinkled sheets half off his waterbed
- another girl's thong still stuck in the box spring
- rust on his sink drain
- a shower curtain he bought from www.Hustler.com
- empty beer bottles stuffed back in the fridge
- empty crates that he uses as a coffee table and end table
- a ratty couch that every time you sit on it, dust balls smack you in the face
- 1000 old rock albums in perfect alphabetical order

We know the guy, because we've either been with this guy, or we are this guy.

Ladies, if you are looking for companionship, read the writing on the wall. If you can find the wall, that is.

If you are looking for a steady companion, no matter how good looking, or rich, or how many times he says, "you're so beautiful, I feel there's something special here," look around and make sure you are with someone who has the same reasons for the date as you.

Is it that easy to know what the other person's reason for the date is?

No. It's never really easy to know. It's hardly that cut and dried. Sometimes you think the other person is on the date for the same reason as you, and it turns out he or she really just wanted sex. That's why the first date should be about fun and getting to know the other person, without getting too intimate. Most women can't handle the aftermath of picking up their undergarments off the floor and hailing a cab at 4:00 A.M.—unless it's the woman's choice. All this unnecessary stress kills the whole purpose of the first date.

WHY IS THE FIRST DATE SO IMPORTANT?

The whole basis of the *Love Connection* show was the first impression.

The first date allows you to judge what kind of person this is:

- Is there an attraction?
- How kind is he or she? How does he or she talk to the waitress? The valet?
- Does he or she have a temper, flip the bird at other drivers?
- Was he or she hours late and didn't call?
- Was he or she ten minutes late and called to let you know he or she was running a little late?
- How does he or she react when someone just took a parking spot you waited fifteen minutes for?

- What does his or her car look like? Clean, cluttered?
- Does this person look you in the eye when he or she talks to you?
- Does this person ask you about yourself?
- Is he or she bad mouthing an ex the whole time? Bad mouthing roommates? Bad mouthing anyone?
- Is he or she making anti-American remarks?
- Does this person work? How does he or she support him- or herself?
- Are there lots of exes or children to support?
- Is he forty and still living with his parents?

REASONS FOR DATING WILL CHANGE ALL THE TIME

The reason the whole dating thing is so complex is because you may be dating just to have fun and meet new and exciting people, and then BOOM, you meet that special someone, and now your reason has changed.

Or you may just want sex, and you truly end up liking this person, and may want him or her to spend the whole night. BOOM...now your reason for the date has changed.

HOW HONEST DO YOU NEED TO BE?

We always hear people telling us to be honest about our intentions so we don't hurt the other person. Honesty takes a lot of guts. Sometimes the easier way out is to run.

Just remember that for the one moment you break out of your own selfish narcissistic narrow world to be honest with someone who may really like you, you can save that person lots of heartache and pain. Be honest, but not overly honest.

If it didn't click...

- Don't imply a second date.
- Don't imply you'll call.
- Don't continue with the compliments.
- Don't have sex.
- Don't drag out the date longer than you have to.
- Don't lie.

You don't have to be too honest. Just be honest enough so you don't mislead that person.

- It's not necessary to tell him that he looks like the *Pillsbury Doughboy*.
- Don't tell her that her voice sounds like a screeching car.
- Don't tell him or her you have a girlfriend or boyfriend, and you're dating just to make him or her jealous.
- Don't tell him or her you really like blondes and the redhead thing isn't doing it for you.
- Don't tell him or her *really* why it's not working out.

The best and safest way is just to say, "Thank you and goodnight."

When he or she says those dreaded words, "So, can I see you again?" just wiggle out of it by saying "I have some things going on in my life. I don't want to mislead you." Leave it at that. If he or she pushes, you can say, "The timing is just not right for me now."

He or she will get over it faster than if you really told the whole truth.

chapter three:

Bouncing Back into Dating

Getting back into dating after being with someone for a long time can be quite frightening and intimidating. No matter what the reason is that you are single again, no matter how old you are, starting over isn't easy.

Whatever you do, don't try to find the exact person you used to be with. They don't exist, unless they were cloned.

The reason that Neil Simon's marriage to Marsha Mason in the play and film *Chapter Two* didn't work was because he was still in love with his first wife, who had died, and he tried to make Marsha Mason the exact replacement. Tragically, you can't do that. Everyone is different. It's a fact of life and science.

If you were dumped, do you know why? It may not hurt to find out so you can learn from that. It may not be anything you did, but if it was, you need to know. Honesty is okay here, because it's someone you've been with.

If you are suddenly alone because your significant other has passed away, this will take more than just this book. Find the support and comfort that helps you through this, and it doesn't always mean hanging out with friends. Just make sure the friends you hang out with aren't too pushy with you to start dating again, especially if you're not ready. Do what's really best for you and your family. It will take time, especially if you had a great relationship before.

If the relationship wasn't good, and was actually quite bad and abusive, this is your out. Seize the moment and start dating again!

Four Common Fears about Getting Back to Dating

1 I'll never meet anyone again.

Not true. There is always someone out there for you. Just make sure you've given yourself enough time to heal before you go back out there. Love can be found with different people, since you are also at a different place in your life.

There are so many more opportunities to meet people. If it was your decision to end your current relationship, then this is your time to really fly and make this time for you. You're probably wiser now. Just make sure you don't settle. Being alone is far better than being with someone you don't really want to be with.

Unfortunately, if it is not your choice to be single for whatever reason, it's not so bad to be alone or with friends for a while. But remember, when the timing is right, and you're ready, you will meet someone again.

They are out there. One hundred million of them.

2 Men only want to date the young babes.

Not true. There are still more men who are look-ing for the special girl that they can relate too. Men pretty much date all women. As long as she's attrac-tive, well groomed, and has sex appeal, age doesn't matter. What if you feel you're not attractive? Then do a makeover. Get yourself to the point that makes you feel attractive and you'll be surprised how that will rub off.

3 Women want the young hunks.

Not true. Women love to look at the young hunks and flirt with them…maybe even have a fling. But women will go for that pot-bellied, bald-headed man, even with the outdated outfit from the '70s, if the man has class—if he opens the door for her, makes her feel like a million bucks, and makes her laugh. Further-more, having a million bucks couldn't hurt either. Women are still more attracted to an average-looking aging man who has money than to a penniless hunk.

4 Women, deep down, want a guy who has money and can take of them.

True. However, if you are a guy and you don't have a lot of money, women can still be swayed if you've got other things going on, such as growth potential at your job, a fledgling stock portfolio, or you know how to meet her emotional needs.

While it is normal to feel intimated by these myths you hear about dating, just remember to take it really slowly. Don't "date" at first. Go on larger get togethers—cruises, parties, sporting events—anywhere there are people who can provide a safe buffer for you. This will give you the opportunity to open up a bit, talk to new people, and slowly get your confidence back.

Don't let your loneliness push you into situations you may regret:

- the One Night Stand (unless you want it)
- a weekend getaway with a jerk
- making a commitment to someone you're not really into
- dating people at work
- sleeping with the boss
- affairs with married people

Ten Ways to Overcome Loneliness

1 **Get a pet.** If you already have one, get another one.

2 **Take courses, like at the Learning Annex.** There are so many fun, interesting courses that will keep you busy.

3 **Do your grocery shopping at night.** Just make sure you have safe parking when you come home.

4 **Go into chat rooms on the computer.** Just know

most of this is a lie, but have fun with it and take it all with a grain of salt.

5 **If you have kids and they're with you, you shouldn't be lonely.** Get to know them again. If they're not with you, make something nice for them. Take up knitting, or some other craft.

6 **Get used to the silence.** It's a good time to reflect on your thoughts.

7 **Start going to socials at your community center or house of worship.** There's always something going on there.

8 **Volunteer.**

9 **Moonlight.** In a club, bar, bowling alley...anywhere that's social where you can have fun.

10 **Get your headset out and listen to books on tape.**

How Dating Has Changed Since You Last Dated

1 **There are many more ways to meet people now.** You've got the Internet, dating services, matchmaking services, and singles events everywhere.

2) **Women are far more open about sex.** If they want it, they'll let you know. They are kinkier, into more games, toys, positions, and adult video making. They'll reveal more about their past relationships, usually more than you want to hear anyway.

3) **Women ask men out.** They are more forward and will offer to pay for things on the date. If the woman asks the man out, it's still nice for the man to pay for the fist date.

4) **The way we listen to music is different.** There are CD's and CD burners. You probably missed the whole music downloading stage, which is good because, for the most part, it's illegal. Go to your local electronics store and see all the new and exciting electronic things we have now. It's fascinating, and most of the things are affordable.

5) **Restaurants are funkier, hipper, and karaoke is everywhere.** There's no excuse to find a dull place to go to.

6) **Sushi, Indian food, and BBQ restaurants are in.** They are fun, and there is something there for all tastes.

7) **Women tend to want to meet in public** rather than

be picked up, especially if it's a blind date set up through the Internet.

8 **The time that dates are set up have changed.** There are more lunch dates, breakfast coffee dates, and dates after work. The Saturday night dinner thing isn't the only time to date.

9 **STDs, HIV, AIDS.** Know about these, and know that they are increasing among young people. Bi-sexuality is more prevalent, and you should be aware of who you are sleeping with.

10 **The way people think has changed.** Since 9/11, people see how fragile life is and want to escape more. More local weekend vacations, more pampering, more going out, and more news watching. People are more afraid. Afraid to go into large crowded areas, over bridges, and under tunnels. *Racial profiling* is the new term for *prejudice.* People are scared, desperate and more vigilant in observing the people around them. They are also quicker to judge, hate, and discriminate. People are more patriotic, more outspoken and passionate about expressing this.

How Dating Hasn't Changed

1. **Women still like the man to pay, hold her door open, help her out of the car, and pull her chair out to help her get seated.** No matter how successful the woman is, being the gentleman is still the way to go. If she's doesn't get it, or appreciate it, then that's a red flag. Always be the gentleman, and you won't lose...at least with the right woman.

2. **Sex is still the first thing on the minds of daters.** How will the date end? If there's lust, sex usually follows. This will never change.

3. **The butterflies you get in your stomach just before you go out.** Dating is a social way for having lots of fun, but also still causes lots of stress and anxiety. Just keep one thing in mind; the other person is just as scared.

Six Ways to Overcome First Date Jitters

Dating fears are for everyone, not just people getting back into dating. You'll find that once you start dating again, the fears won't be as intense, because you will start to develop a sense of confidence

1. **Have a friend set you up to go out with a group of people.** You'll have people to lean on when in doubt.

2 **Keep the first date short and simple.** There are so many great coffee shops all over the place, at almost every corner. There is so much to learn about that person in one hour that will determine if it's worth spending another hour together.

And, you can quickly observe inappropriate behavior. For example, if he doesn't have money to pay for your coffee, either he's a cheap bastard, or a poor one. Either way…not for you. And if she shows up with her six kids, you can cut the date to ten minutes. That's how long it will take you to get all their names right and run.

3 **Be ready for small talk.** There are lots of great "getting to know you" questions in this book.

4 **Have lots of phone conversations.** This way when you meet it will be like you already know that person.

5 **Email each other.** Just remember that words can be misinterpreted, so don't get too cutesy, or you may turn that person off.

6 **Remember that you are loveable.** It's happened before, it will happen again. Don't let anyone take that away from you. Now get out there and have some fun.

chapter four:

The Pre-Date Makeover

It's normal to have first-date jitters. Anything that is new will bring on all sorts of insecurities.

"What will that person think of me?"

"What if she turns out to be a real wacko?"

"What if I'm attracted to my date, and he doesn't seem attracted to me?"

"What if this is a great person, and I'm just not attracted? I don't want to hurt anyone's feelings."

What if, what if, what if?

Here Are Some Tips to Calm You Down That Really Do Work

1 **It's only one date, not a lifelong commitment.** Keep it in perspective.

2 **Remember that we're all human.** We all came from the same place and are going to the same place. Only in different outfits.

3 **Know that the other person is just as nervous as you.**

④ **Look as fabulous as you can.** This way you'll feel confident and know you put your best foot forward.

⑤ **If you're truly having a bad time, cut the date short.** Don't ever feel obligated to anyone but yourself.

Getting Your Head Together

Get rid of negative influences in your life.

① **Family.** Well, you can't really get rid of them, but don't hang around them too often if it means your self-esteem is shot all the time. You don't need constant reminders that Weight Watchers is having another lifetime member sale.

② **Friends.** You don't want to get rid of all of them, only the ones who make you feel like a loser every time you're with them. Women can be catty, bitchy, and phony. Some of them want to see you fail because it makes them feel better about their own failures.

The true test of a sincere friend is to see who sticks by you when you transform yourself in the person you want to be and find that special someone to share it with. That's the friend that will be there to hold your bouquet.

3 **Co-workers.** You can't really get rid of them unless you switch jobs, and then there will be other co-workers. Just keep your mouth shut. People talk about their love lives too much at work. You don't need their advice, unless you truly have a loyal friend to share your feelings with after work. The worst thing to hear all day from a co-worker is sympathy over your dating failures.

4 **Psychology Books.** Dump them. They are a constant reminder of how messed up you "think" you are. If you truly are "messed up" you should be seeking professional help. Hospitals and 24-hour help hot lines are available. If you're not really all that messed up, then you don't need all those books.

5 **Photographs of your past around your home that conjure up sadness,** especially if you're widowed, dumped, or have moved away. Fill your living space with happy things. Surround yourself with scenery, abstract art, animation—anything that will make you smile. If mementos cause you to cry every time you come home, you won't be in a dating frame of mind.

6 **Your alter ego.** The one that tells you you're a fat, ugly loser. The one that tells you you'll never meet anyone because you talk too much, don't know anything about world politics, and can't cook. The one

that tells you all the good ones are taken. It's time to say goodbye to that person. You truly are fine. You just need to make some alterations.

7 **Get your body physically fit.** This doesn't mean working out for hours a day. It means adding a little more physical activity to your day. Walk or bike instead of driving. Take the stairs instead of the elevator. Join a gym and walk on the treadmill for twenty minutes, three times a week. You'll feel energized and ready to go.

8 **Get enough sleep.** If you stay up all night in chat rooms, get up early for work, and then go out on a date, you'll be exhausted. That's not fair to you and not fair to your date.

9 **Eat right.** That doesn't mean cutting out your Big Macs. That means if you are going to gorge yourself with four billion calories, add some fruit, yogurt, something healthy. You truly are what you eat, and flab and gas don't go well romantically.

10 **Watch those herbs, weight-loss products, and vitamins.** Most of them are a waste of money. Don't overdo it. You may be hurting yourself in the long run. Consult with a doctor—that means a real doctor. Not the guy with the white coat in an herb store trying

to sell you a pack of unsubstantiated claims. If you're into alternative medicine, find a naturopath with an H.D. degree or consult a dietician.

GETTING YOUR HOME READY

If your date is picking you up from your place, then the first impression begins even before your date sets eyes on you. I heard numerous times at *Love Connection* how "we had great phone conversation and I was excited for the date. But when I walked up to my date's home, I had to climb over mountains of garbage, as if I were in a junkyard. I wondered, 'What kind of pig is this?'"

You can spend all day getting yourself looking beautiful, but you will be judged on the cleanliness of your living space as well. If you live with roommates, kids, or parents, make sure their junk is out of the way, too. First impressions apply to everything around you.

Here is a checklist of how to prepare your home:

- Get rid of nasty smells. Take out the garbage, repair the plumbing, and dehumidify moldy spaces.
- Open windows to air the place out.
- Give your place a thorough cleaning.
- Burn candles, but not strong incense, because that could be too overwhelming. Keep scents light and simple.
- Stock your refrigerator. Include fresh milk, eggs, bread, a few pieces of fruit, cheese and crackers, fruit juice, and coffee. You never know whether

you'll be serving a midnight snack or a morning-after repast.

- Remove anything embarrassing from your medicine cabinet. Your date will snoop.
- Make sure your answering machine is turned down low, so you can protect your privacy.
- Make sure any porn magazines or videos are tucked away.
- Make sure the pets are tucked away. Not everyone is into Fido jumping all over. It really isn't that cute.
- Make sure the kids are tucked away safely...preferably at grandma's house. Even if they're sleeping, it's hard to get romantic when you could be interrupted at any moment.

GETTING YOUR CAR/VEHICLE READY

First of all, if you're a man, make sure you have a vehicle. Unless you don't for medical or age reasons, it's a *red flag* if you are picking up your date by bus or tractor-trailer. Motorcycles are cool if your date knows about it in advance.

You don't have to drive a Mercedes, but whatever car/truck you have, you should clean it up. During my interviews with *Love Connection* contestants, another complaint would be how messy the car was. That indicated a messy person. One girl told me about used condoms, smelly jock straps, and porn magazines in the back of her date's car. That turned her off the whole night, and the date was cut short.

Don't rent an expensive car, or borrow one just to show off to your date. If the two of you click and you continue going out your date will feel deceived when you pull up in your beat-up jalopy. You would have been better off pulling up in your old jalopy in the first place and risking your date being turned off by the car rather than killing off a budding relationship because you were deceitful.

Remember, if a woman is turned off by you because you don't have a fancy, expensive car, then she's not for you, and there was nothing you could have done. If a woman is turned off by you because you deceived her, then she could have been right for you and you blew it.

FOOLPROOF WAYS TO MAKE A GREAT FIRST IMPRESSION: APPEALING TO YOUR FIVE SENSES

Outer Appearance: The New You

Some of you may say, "I don't need a makeover. If they don't like me for who I am, then I don't want them." Sound familiar?

This attitude needs to change. Every human being can use a makeover every now and then. It's part of living, part of keeping up with the times. Some of you take better care of your car, home, trailer, boat, home entertainment center, or computer than of yourself.

Not only can looks be deceiving, *they are deceiving.*

The real you—the funny one, the smart one, the sexy one—may be hidden behind your outdated mullet cut, or the extra ten pounds you're carrying.

Time to dump your '80s wardrobe and your Peter Frampton locks. (Even Peter dumped his Peter Frampton locks.) Time to hit Macy's, Wal-Mart, Payless, or the outlet malls. Time to invest in some new clothes.

It takes the mind three to six seconds to form a first impression. Please be aware that if the other person isn't attracted to you, after you've gone to the trouble of making yourself over, then there's nothing you could have done. It all goes back to the whole initial chemistry thing. It can't be analyzed. It's just the way it is. But at least you know that you did your best to make yourself look the best you could. That's what counts.

At *Love Connection* I heard hundreds of times, "I really liked her. She was pretty, well mannered, well groomed, great figure, nice teeth, nice shoes, nice job, nice car, nice...everything."

But it didn't click.

It goes back to the chemistry thing. There is no escaping it.

The whole dating scene is a numbers game. You should be selective and date as many people as you can until you meet the one that's right for you.

Don't settle for the guy with the great looks, great body, great job, great house, great health insurance plan, great 401k plan, and great summerhouse in the Hamptons, if you see the red flags. Those red flags can save you years of heartache, pain, and time if you're open to them.

Don't settle for that gorgeous babe in the size three jeans, the one who takes you for every dime on a date. The one who orders the most expensive thing on the menu while giving the cute waiter more eye contact than you. If she's doing this now, just wait and see what she'll do to you ten years later in divorce court.

First Date Red Flags

Red flags are so important because they are the things that help shape your first impression of the person you're going out with. The beginning of the date will be loaded with red flags ready to bust out at any given moment. As you get to know the person, those red flags may either multiply or diminish as you start developing your feelings more.

Behavioral Traits That Trigger Red Flags:

- rude
- temperamental
- yells at people
- lies
- cheats
- late
- doesn't have money in his wallet but drives a Porsche
- talks about the kids too much
- talks about the ex too much
- complains too much
- doesn't stop talking

- doesn't talk at all
- sloppy
- out of work, with access to a trust account
- moves a lot
- stares too much at the waiter or waitress
- reveals too much about a kinky past
- takes you shopping for expensive things
- doesn't greet you with anything
- poor table manners
- snores during a movie (Could have a medical condition. Find out what it is.)
- keeps reminding you "I'm not ready to get serious"

Red flags are first date gold mines for really seeing who this person is. Don't ignore them. No one is perfect. There are red flags you can live with, and red flags that will drive you crazy.

You'll know what you can live with and what will drive you crazy. You'll know because the pit of your stomach will remind you.

If it doesn't click for you, if you're not attracted, if the chemistry isn't working for you, don't stick around. Because if he ever loses those looks, job, body, or insurance plan you'll feel stuck and may have missed other opportunities with the *right* guy.

Look the best you can, and date as much as you can.

Build it...it will come!

Twelve Ways to Improve Your Appearance: What You Need To Invest In

1 **Get your weight where you want it.** If you've always wanted to lose five pounds, now's the time. How good you feel about yourself will definitely show when you first meet someone. If you can't afford to go to Weight Watchers or other groups, there are plenty of diets on the Internet. Consult with your physician to make sure you find the right healthy program for you. This is the first and best investment to make. You'll feel healthier and sexier.

2 **Get a new hair cut.** The balding guy with the long ponytail in a rubber band is rather disgusting. Do you really think a ponytail can cover up your big bald head?

Women, get a nice, shiny do. If you're over sixteen years old and still have hair below your waist, then get it cut. Hint: There are beauty schools that offer great deals to the public.

3 **Clear away unwanted hair.** From your face, your armpits, your nose, your ears—and that goes for men, too. A man doesn't like a woman to have more hair than he does, unless it's on her head. Women don't like to touch a man's back with a jungle of hair growing out of it (may I suggest waxing?).

4 **Fix your teeth.** Or at least, if you are missing some, get them in. It's worth the investment.

5 **Modernize your clothes.** This doesn't mean going out to Nordstrom's and blowing $5,000. But with all the sales going on all the time, get some basic clothes that are timeless and attractive. The jeans torn at the knees are rather disgusting.

6 **Clean your fingernails.** If you're all dolled up in your new suit and you've got filthy nails, you might as well pack it in now.

7 **Length of nails.** Guys, it's okay to get a manicure. Women love men with trim nails, and clear polish works. Women should also make sure the length of their acrylic nails isn't longer than his penis is likely to be. That could hurt. It's also not all that attractive.

8 **Shoes.** Make sure they match and are clean. At *Love Connection*, shoes were the first thing women looked at to judge a guy. Flip-flops that expose a guy's big hairy toes don't contribute to that sexy look.

9 **Accessories.** Don't go out looking like a walking flea market. Too many "tchotchke" things—belts, clips, broaches—are a distraction, and could get in the way of that later goodnight kiss. Big, bold, clunky earrings,

bracelets, or toe rings make you look cheap. Less is more. Less is classy. Less makes a good first impression.

10 **Body piercings, tattoos.** In a normal, civilized world, too much of anything doesn't work. That goes for the statements you're trying to make by wearing anti-government tattoos all over your body or the fifteen earrings in one ear. If you know for a fact your date is into all this body art, then that's different. But don't assume that just because you and your friends love having every morsel of your skin tattooed or pierced that your date will too. This doesn't make a good first impression. If you still want to maintain the "fairy tale" philosophy and say, "they have to take me for what I am," then good luck!

11 **Feet.** Men, this goes for you, too. It's okay to get a pedicure. You can shine from head to ankle, but if your feet are gross it will take more than a dinner at Coco's to remove that memory from your date's head. Ladies, the same goes for you. Check your feet to make sure your calluses, corns, or blisters from poorly fitting shoes are covered. Men truly love to see women in open-toe sandals, with sexy polish. It's worth the investment.

12 **The whole look.** Putting it all together. Make sure your whole look, the entire package (that's you), is

dressed for the place you are going to.

Too often at *Love Connection* people complained that their date was too dressy for cycling, or too casual for a fine dining restaurant. Understand what the plans are. If it's a "surprise" date, then dress in between and bring a nice change of clothing to put in the car. Pack some toiletries as well, so you can freshen up.

The way you put your whole package together can make or break your first impression. You should know...you also make these judgements.

Sense of Smell

1 **Take a shower.** Believe it or not, another complaint was that people went on their dates still sweaty from whatever they had been doing.

2 **Your breath.** If you know you have a date coming up, avoid garlic, raw onions, and strong spices before. These odors tend to linger not only in your mouth, but through the pores of your skin as well. Chew on bread or parsley, which will cleanse your mouth, and bring mints with you.

3 **Your skin scent.** Be very careful not to mix cologne or perfume with perfumed soap or lotion (unless

the scents are all from the same family). A strong perfumed aroma is a turn off. Go light, and gently re-apply later.

4 **Your feet.** Make sure that when you take your shoes off they don't smell. If you notice it, your date will too.

5 **Your hair.** Men love running their hands through a woman's hair, and women love caressing a man's scalp. It's unappealing when your date is in a romantic mood and clumps of greasy hairballs fall into the palm of his or her hand. Don't overdo the spray to cover up the fact that you haven't washed your hair in a week. It's the law of hygiene. Always have freshly washed hair and a clean scalp.

6 **Armpits.** No matter how much you take a shower or put powder on, there is nothing on the market like anti-perspirants for your underarms. The deodorants that you buy in the health food stores are good for smell, but not for sweat. Wet sweat marks under your armpits can lead to smelliness.

Your initial scent can ruin what would have otherwise been a great first impression. You don't need to spend lots of money on this. In our society there is no excuse for smelliness.

Sound

1 **Your voice.** There's not much you can change about this. If you sound like Daffy Duck or any other cartoon character, then you better have everything else going for you. Your sound, especially if it's out of the ordinary, can make a great first impression go sour.

2 **Your laugh.** I've seen people get dumped just for their laugh. If a woman has a loud cackle (you know who you are), most men don't like it. However, some men find this exhilarating. But try to control the cackle if you can. That also goes for the grunt, the snort, or the squeal laugh. Be conscious of your laugh.

3 **Your cry.** If you're seeing a movie or play where it's dark, quiet, and calm and you start wailing like a two-year-old whose cookie has been taken, that sound can be quite a turn-off. Whimpering, or anything too extreme, can break the moment. Keep your crying to a soft, subtle sound. That goes for you ladies too.

Sense of Taste

1 **Your kiss.** The taste of your kiss is so important. You can have it all going for you, but if you taste like a

carton of sour milk, it's hard to win that person over again. Don't be shy to pull out mints or spray before the kiss. You're better off doing that than risking a sour taste.

2 **Your body.** That's why the shower thing is so important. Unless you're made of plastic, the body sweats and has odor naturally. This goes for your feet as well. Lotions may smell nice, but taste bad. Use perfumed soap, or specially made scents that are made for tasting, and taste it yourself. A simple sucking of your arm or hand should do. If it's bitter to you, it will be worse for the other person.

3 **The forgotten tasting zone: your ears.** Waxy plaque in your ears can taste like a horse's ass. (Not that anyone that I know of has tasted a horse's ass, but if you judge a taste by its smell, then you know what I mean. Although I never really smelled a horse's ass, either.) If you judge the smell by what you can imagine it to be, you'll really know what I mean. Clean your ears and apply nice smelling lotion, or a quick spritz of cologne.

4 **The ultimate tasting zone** (not really meant for a first date, but be ready just in case): your genital areas. Your thighs, butt, penis, vagina, the whole cake. It doesn't hurt to wash up again in any restroom during the date, and always keep that area fresh,

clean, and tasting like candy. Putting some candy on couldn't hurt either. Just make sure to use sugar free if your date is a diabetic.

Sense of Touch

1 **Smooth skin.** Try to get your skin as smooth as you can if you're a lady. You can't help moles or birthmarks, and when you start touching, you can guide your date's hand away from those sensitive areas if you wish. For men, women like to touch a man's strong skin, but if your back is hairy and pimply that can be a turn-off. Many spas offer what is essentially a facial for your back. It will make a big difference.

2 **Smooth face.** Women love to look at a guy's sexy goatee, but touching massive hair on a face can itch, scratch, and detract from the romantic mood. Men also don't like to caress a woman's face that has stubble. Touch your face and see how it feels to you. If it doesn't feel smooth, you need more shaving, plucking, or waxing. Once again, if it's a skin problem that is hard to fix, try to avoid having your date touch those areas on the first date.

3 **Smooth private parts.** Men don't like to touch a woman's nipples that have hair coming out of them.

You can trim these hairs, if plucking scares you. Make sure your genital areas are smoothly shaven. Women also get grossed out by a man's excessively hairy ass. Feel your ass. If it seems like soft hair, then that's fine. If it's coarse, and you have mounds of it, try a professional waxing.

Now that you've completely made yourself over from head to toe, including your home, your car, and your head, how do you feel—sexy, hip, and fabulous?

5 Ways to Feel Sexy, Hip, And Fabulous

For Women

1. **Wear sexy undergarments.**

2. **Don't eat too much that day.** Eat healthy to give you energy, so if you're going for the McNuggets, leave out the fries. Carbs can bloat you, and you won't feel sexy.

3. **Pick an outfit that's sexy.** Black works and men love jeans. I don't care if you are a professional woman. Leave your "suit" at the office, and put on something shimmery, soft, and sexy.

4. **Wear sexy shoes.** Clunky clogs or sneakers won't make you feel sexy. Something with a sandal look, heels, nicely painted toes, even with jeans will work.

5 **Keep your breath feeling fresh.** Having a clean, fresh mouth, with mints or gum handy, will put you in a kissing mood (providing you want to kiss).

For Men

1 **Shower, groom yourself.**

2 **Don't overdo the eating that day,** and stay away from too much drinking, and carbs. Carbs create gas, and having that gassy feeling on a date won't make you feel sexy.

3 **Put on your best fitting pants, and most comfortable shirt,** providing they are in good condition. Anything too tight around your balls lends itself to an unsexy feeling.

4 **Act manly.** Even if the woman seems really independent, hold the door open for her, pull out her chair, and open her car door. If you act the part, you'll feel the part.

5 **Have extra money in your pocket.** Don't squash your sexy feeling by not having enough money in your pocket to tip the waiter or buy your date a rose.

Now, you're ready to date.

chapter five:

75 Proven Places to Find A Date

Singles everywhere, no matter what age they are, love to discover new and exciting places to meet new people.

Do these statements sound familiar?

"There are no decent single men."

"All the women I meet are bitches."

"The guys I meet are so immature."

"All a woman wants is a guy with a trust fund."

You need to recognize that this may seem true, but don't let it stop you. Rarely does anything in life come easy. If it does, there is a price to pay somewhere. This is a fact. The bigger truth here is that there are lots of nice single men, and not all women are bitches. You just need to keep getting out there.

There are many reasons why you may not be meeting people to date, one of which is you're not putting yourself out there. That means getting out more. It's very easy to get into the rut of going to work, coming home, and lying on the couch. Or you may be a single parent and you're with the kids all day. Unless you date the pizza delivery man or your neighbor you are limiting your chances of finding a date.

GETTING STARTED

If you are ready, truly ready to date, then the first step is to *alter the pattern of your life, your daily routine*. For example:

If you like to do your paperwork in front of the TV, try putting it in a box and taking it over to a coffee shop.

If you have newspapers to get caught up with, try going to a hotel lobby, or bar/restaurant.

Bring your household mail, favorite book, or magazines and get busy in places where you have the chance to meet people.

Here Is a proven List of Places to go Where You Can Meet People.

1 **Crash a party.** Especially in hotels, or banquet halls. This takes nerve, but it truly is fun. Get dressed up, walk in like you know someone, head over to the bar area, and start mingling. The best excuse for being here is that you're scouting the room for a future party you plan on throwing.

2 **Go to as many parties as you are invited to.** Throw one yourself—for the heck of it. Make up a fun reason, too, like on a Sunday night, have a "Bring one item from your fridge party," or a "Bring one item of clothing that you've had for years and won't part with party." Any reason will do.

3 **Bars.** It's a myth that you don't meet anyone decent there. Just make sure the person you're connecting with isn't falling off his barstool. If you're that person, then it's time to take a cab home.

4 **Moonlighting.** Take a second job. Pick a place where you have the chance to meet someone, like a sporting goods store, a pub, or a catering company where you'll work lots of parties. Avoid places like nursing homes, mental institutions, kindergarten classrooms, or overnight security desks.

5 **Art gallery gathering.** Check your local paper for show times, or call nearby galleries and ask them when their next opening is. It's a great way to mingle and chug back some free wine.

6 **Author book signing.** These are great mingling functions, icebreakers, and casual functions. Even if you don't know who the author is, you can scope the place out. Beware of authors who are promoting books on depression, suicide, or infidelity. Fans of these books may not be the kind you want to date.

7 **Volunteer somewhere.** A hospital, fund-raiser, or community event always needs volunteers. Even if you have to wear a stupid uniform, make sure everything else on you is properly groomed.

8 **Electronics store.** Hang out in the home stereo department. It's more social. Do this experiment yourself. Watch people who are spending all their time with the headsets on in the "walkman" department. They seem pretty sterile. People who are into home stereos, the bigger stuff, have bigger dreams. Bigger pockets don't hurt either.

9 **Beauty salon/barber shop.** Schedule your appointments during busy times, where you probably have to wait. It gives you time to check things out more. Be careful to not spill your heart out too much to the stylists. They will blab your secrets. It's not a good idea to complain that you never meet anyone in the same breath that you talk about how much you hate yourself.

10 **Flea market/street fair.** Bring some cash here. It can be a great place for conversation starters. If you spot someone interesting, follow him or her around to see whom he or she is with, what he or she buys, and most of all how he or she talks to the help.

11 **Car wash.** You may need to splurge every now and then and go to places where you sit and wait for your car. Do-it-yourself car washes, where you stand there with your own hose, aren't the best places to meet someone. They're for people who have no money, or

who are cheap, or are too anal or picky to go to a real car wash. Is this dating material for you?

12 **Anywhere there is food.** Try the mall, restaurants, or fast food joints. Where food goes, people will follow. But don't sit there and stuff your face. It's unattractive to be shoving mounds of fries in your face when you're on the "prowl" (unless you're a size three or under twenty-one).

13 **The laundromat.** Pick one in an upscale neighborhood. Make sure you don't bring your ratty, stained underwear. Ladies, it is sexy for men to see what you wear to bed, so if you want to throw in some sexy lingerie for the heck of it, go for it.

14 **The supermarket.** Pick one in a decent neighborhood. Use this time to read the magazines at the check out. Nothing better than checking out your groceries at the same time you're checking out your Saturday night date!

15 **A food tasting.** Read your local paper to find out where free tastings are taking place. They are usually at the grocery store or smaller gourmet markets. The hors d'oeuvres make great conversation starters.

16 **Bingo.**

17 **Dance lessons.** Tango, salsa, ballroom—any dance. Not only is it a great night out, but there's nothing sexier than a man who knows how to take the lead on the dance floor. Remember, *dating is one long dance*. Start with some lessons.

18 **Bridge or other card game groups.** If you know how to play these games, join a group. If you don't know the game, then you can really piss people off by slowing down the play (unless you're a size three or under twenty-one), so take some lessons first.

19 **Learning Annex, or a community college course.** It may sound boring—going back to school—but there are so many new exciting courses from wine tasting to home repair. Find something that interests you. It's a sure way to meet others with the same interests.

20 **Luncheon/breakfast counter.** This can be a great place to talk to the waiter/waitress and have him or her help you meet someone if you're too shy to make the approach. You won't feel so alone either.

21 **Sports bar.** Constant party atmosphere can be found here. Even if your team loses, it's another reason to pour another.

22 **Sporting event.** Different events attract different kinds of people. You probably won't see the same guy who goes to monster truck competitions show up at a polo match. Try as many as you can. It will be a learning experience and allow you to be experimental.

23 **Sporting goods store.** Hanging out in the swimming section is better for guys meeting women, and women should hang out in the "macho" sports sections.

24 **Playing sports.** Join a co-ed baseball team, bowling team, or fencing club. Even if you suck at it, at least you're out there.

25 **Fashion show.** Men can check out fashion shows. In today's age, women know that you're there for one of two reasons: you may be gay, or you are there to check out the women. Either way, you're going to be an object of interest.

26 **Reunion.** Don't worry if they're not even yours. Anytime there's a reunion, there are people who want to check other people out. Pick a school like Harvard, Columbia, or Princeton—whatever is your style—look them up on the Internet and see if there's a reunion coming up.

27 **Hotel bar.** Great social atmosphere and very playful.

Just note that you may meet someone who is looking for a one-nighter.

28 **Convention/trade show.** These places are all about talking and meeting people. Check for wedding bands, and be aware that the people in the booths are there to sell, so make your approach when things slow down.

29 **Church/synagogue.** You don't have to be religious to attend these functions, but it wouldn't hurt to attend a place of worship of your own faith. Why complicate things?

30 **Fitness center.** You can join two kinds. One to really work out at and get sweaty, and one for socialization. It's worth the investment. There are lots of small, great gyms at affordable prices that allow you to lose weight at one, while gaining a date at another. Looks are important at all times. Save your really sweaty and smelly workout for the other gym. (Unless you're a size three or under twenty-one.)

31 **Weekend getaway.** Go alone or with a friend. If your friend is way more attractive than you are, you're better off going alone.

32 **Cruise.** There are lots of shorter weekend cruises at great prices.

33 **Home and garden show.** With the popularity of home improvement shows such as *Trading Places*, these kinds of shows are great for meeting people with your interests.

34 **Exotic car show.** These shows can be boring if you're not into cars, but it's still worth a shot for meeting a potential date.

35 **Discussion group/PTA/Homeowner's Association meeting.** If you are the argumentative type, then here's your place. Nothing like getting into bitter arguments with people even before the relationship starts.

36 **Elevator.** If you don't like to stare at the other person's shoes, and he or she seems cute, make eye contact. You only have seconds to make your move, so now's not the time to hesitate.

37 **Music shop.** Great way to check out the musical tastes of others. Natural conversation starters can be, "Can you hum the music to this song?"

38 **Book store.** If you spot someone you like the looks of, check out the books he or she is reading to see if your interests are compatible. If they are, it's an instant topic of conversation. On the other hand, if he or she is in the gay/lesbian section, and you're

straight, this may not be a person to approach. The chances that a person is in that section to do research are one in a billion.

39 **Amusement park.** These places are full of party atmosphere. Try to sit in the same car as the cute person you spotted. This is a place to scream for joy without having to put on a condom.

40 **Magazine stand.** Buy at least one thing here, or you may overstay your welcome—unless you're a size three or under twenty-one.

41 **24-hour diner.** If you're ever feeling lonely and are about to sleep with someone you don't want to or call that abusive ex, then escape to a diner. You're better off eating a pound of fries smothered with gravy than shacking up for the night with someone you don't want to be with. Remember you're here to check out the other people—you may meet someone interesting who works the night shift.

42 **Race track.** This gets a bad rap. What's so wrong with blowing a paycheck on horses and beer once in a while? You've got to live it up. Try and schmooze your way into the VIP section by pretending to be a reporter from the "Times." Be sure to check out the winner's circle.

43 **Casino/gambling joint**. Ladies, hit the high roller tables where either smart rich men are, or stupid poor people. The way to tell is to look at a person's shoes. Get all dressed up and pick your target. Body language is crucial here. If you see you're not getting any response—even eye contact—move on. Gamblers are very superstitious, and if there is a chance you are good luck for them, they will make eye contact with you.

44 **Gas stations.** Ladies, if you see someone interesting, ask him or her how to open your tank. There is nothing like pumping your car and testosterone at the same time.

45 **Computer store.** Computer nerds can be really sexy.

46 **Fishing tackle store.** If you ever wanted to learn how to hook a fish and a date at the same time, this is the place. Just stay away from sharks.

47 **Video/DVD rental store.** Great place for single parents to meet single parents, especially on a Friday night.

48 **Library.** For the most part this can be a boring place to go, but most libraries have special events with authors that will attract interesting people.

49 **Daredevil stuff.** Try skydiving, bungee jumping,

windsurfing, scuba diving, racecar driving, or hot air ballooning. If you have life insurance, then fly away.

50 **Happy hour.** You can find free food, cheap drinks, and fun atmosphere. Pick a happy hour that isn't in a family-style restaurant.

51 **Dog walking.** It's worth buying a dog for this. There's nothing like being set up on a date by Fido and Fifi.

52 **Children's hangout.** *Please, only if you're there with your children.* It's freaky for people who don't have kids to go to Gymboree or kid flicks. *If you're not with your kid, this is not a good choice.* You have seventy-four other places to choose from.

53 **Night school.** Take courses that interest you. There are so many exciting courses available now. Find something that gets you excited—and check out the instructors while you're at it.

54 **Live demonstration.** Gatherings attract people. People like to mingle here. County fairs, malls, and supermarkets all have interesting pitch people showing off useless gadgets.

55 **Shopping mall.** This is a great place to escape when you're feeling lonely. At the very least, you can treat

yourself to a nice gift. But browse the men's department first.

56 **Auto repair shop.** This is where women feel the most uncomfortable. But there's nothing like meeting a cute guy to talk to while your tires are being rotated.

57 **Investment seminar.** Not only do these places attract lots of people from all walks of life, but you may learn something. Just don't get racked into spending money on their books and tapes, if you truly feel you won't use them. You're going because it's social, and you can pick up some tips.

58 **Golf club.** If you really enjoy golf, this is a good place. If you hate golf, it's not a good idea. Golfers are very passionate about this sport, and if you started dating and it eventually came out that you find golf to be as boring as watching a clock, you will have started the date on a false note.

59 **Outdoor concert.** There's nothing like fresh air, great music, and a bottle of wine to unwind. Bring an extra bottle to send over to the girls sitting on the next blanket.

60 **Block party.** These are great for single parents. Kids are a great way to meet other parents. Even if you

meet married couples, they usually know someone. Set ups are still the easiest way to meet.

61 **Pet store.** If you don't have human friends to set you up, then pet stores are a great place to meet people. It's fun, makes for great conversation, and you may want to check out who the vet is in the back.

62 **Pool hall.** If you don't play pool, it's even better. A good pool player would love to show you some tricks. Pool halls are sexy, flirtatious, and attract all types, from blue collar to professionals.

63 **Karaoke night.** No matter how old you are, karaoke is one non-stop frat party. It's the only place in the world, other than your best friend's wedding, that you can get up on stage drunk, mess up the all-time classic hit "You Light Up My Life," and get a standing ovation.

64 **Traffic.** Look around you and see if there is anyone interesting.

65 **Form your own book or movie review club or any other club that interests you.** Each person has to bring another single person, and you can rotate the location. This is can provide a great, easy excuse for getting to meet people, and learning about them as well, without having to worry about the goodnight kiss.

66 Wine tasting. Who cares about labels, swooshing the glass around, sediment, and color? All you have to care about at a wine tasting is which wine gives you the best buzz so you can talk to people. Keep it light, though; you'll look like an idiot if you get smashed here.

67 Cooking club. Another great, fun, sexy way to meet people. Here you can share your favorite recipes and really gauge another person. The way a person cooks reveals if he or she is a control freak, the sharing type, or a time bomb ready to go off. It's a great place to observe character.

68 Day spa. You'll get to relax here at the same time you're chatting up good-looking people in the lounge. And people who come to spas tend to have higher incomes, so the prospects are good.

69 Lines. Any line will do. Try lines at the supermarket, movies, or lotto. Lines are great for testing out a few of your own lines.

70 Country and Western line dancing groups.

71 Matinee (movie or live theatre). Usually people come here alone, or with another person who is either wealthy, on shift work, or out of work. Either way, someone isn't working and if you do strike up conversation at a weekday matinee, then you do want to find out as quickly as possible how they got out of work to come.

72 **Weight loss classes**, such as Weight Watchers or Jenny Craig. This can be the best place to meet someone who truly shares your same interests and goals. These places allow for you to be open about yourself in a setting that's comfortable for talking about your innermost thoughts.

73 **Brunch place.** You get free champagne and lots of great food with a really festive atmosphere.

74 **Home improvement centers,** like Home Depot or Lowe's. This is like a cooking class, where you truly are in a setting that is specific to your interest. Home decorating and building are topics that people can go on and on about, and you can really get a sense of personalities and tastes.

75 **Your own backyard.** Check out your neighbors. Your dream date may be just around the corner.

Singles are everywhere. With a one hundred million out there, you are bound to meet someone soon. Use this list.

Please note that as a single person, you must always be "on" if you are truly serious about meeting someone.

BASICS

Here Are the Staples You'll Need
Every Time You Leave Your Place:

1 **Look decent every time you go out.** You never know when that chance meeting will happen.

2 **Always carry a pen and paper.** You'll need it to write down phone numbers.

3 **Always carry mints.** You could be close to someone in the supermarket line, and still have that garlic smell on your breath.

4 **Be informed.** Have some general knowledge about the news of the day. Most guys like to start off the day with something in the headlines. The only topic a woman is allowed to be ignorant of is sports scores. But you should know who our President is, and what his wife's name is.

5 **Keep a change of clothing in the trunk of your car.** If you meet someone terrific, you'll want to freshen up.

THE BLIND DATE
The whole concept at *Love Connection* was the blind date. Singles wanted to find others who were already

checked out by someone they knew and trusted. The traditional "set up" is a tactic that has worked for decades. Marriages were arranged by families even before the bride and groom knew each other. In some cultures this method is still being used.

No matter how many miserable blind dates you may have had, it's still worth it. You never know if this is the person you'll end up with. Keep getting set up and keep going out. It's still better to have unsuccessful dates than none at all. You'll make better conversation at the office the next day talking about how the guy you went out with ran out of gas, took you to the morgue to identify a relative, and had the hiccups all night. Or you can talk about what a great couch you have.

Who Blind Dates Are *Not* For:
- Blind dates are not for losers, as some may think.
- Blind dates are not for married people.
- Blind dates are not for people who think that the reason people go on blind dates is because they aren't good enough to find someone on their own.
- Blind dates are not for people who have no sense of adventure.
- Blind dates may not be for you.

Who Blind Dates *Are* For
- Blind dates are for people with open minds, who feel if there's no attraction, "next."

- Blind dates are for people who won't blame anyone afterwards if the date sucks. You still want them to continue setting you up.
- Blind dates are for people who want to get out of a dating rut.
- Blind dates are for those who are tired of being lonely.
- Blind dates are for those who still love a great mystery and hold on to the hope that this special person is out there.
- Blind dates are probably for you.

Three Great Advantages of the Blind Date

1 Gives you a chance to meet all kinds of people: the good, the bad, and the ugly.

2 You can use the experience as a way to learn how to gauge people, as well as yourself.

3 You have a date.

Six Tips on Getting People to Fix You Up

1 **Tell them you'd like to be fixed up.** Put out the word to everyone you know, doctors, bankers, people at work, neighbors, and some family—but don't sound desperate.

People, other than family, fly away from desperation and you don't want project that image, even if it's true.

2   **Tell them not to make you sound desperate,** as if it's been really hard for you to find a date. In innocence, your "do gooder" friends may come across over zealous and sabotage the whole thing.

3   **Tell them to not reveal too many personal things in your life,** like that your father was just arrested for making a bomb in the basement of your home, or that you're getting over an abortion. It's not necessary for a blind date.

Tell them the kind of person you'd like to date.
4   Explain the qualities you are looking for, such as someone who has a steady job and nice shoes. Don't hold back if you really want someone who has a house in the country, a condo in the city, a country club membership, and a trust account. Why settle for less if you can afford not to? But if you find yourself still single and searching at age seventy, then you may want to give a little on the nice shoes.

5   **Tell them that after the date you don't want to be grilled.** No matter what they tell you, you can be guaranteed that everything you say about this person will get back to him or her.

6 **Tell them you won't hold them accountable if the person turns out to be a real dud.** Sometimes people hold back on fixing others up because they don't want to be responsible for a lousy time and hurt your friendship. You're going into it with an open mind. However, if the same person fixes you up more than twice with a loser, then you may want to think carefully before having him or her fix you up with anyone else.

chapter six:

Hot New Dating Alternatives

For people who work, finding time to date can be a real hassle. It is a fact that the average worker spends close to twelve hours a day working, including the commute. Weekends are filled with chores, family, and friends. When time is so valuable singles have turned to the two hottest dating alternatives that are growing every day.

Speed Dating and Internet/online dating seem to be the new rage. While true romantics argue that the whole romance thing is taken away, it isn't stopping the millions upon millions of daters from continuing to use this method. Even though the fear here is that this is a system based on strangers meeting strangers, perhaps this is part of the romance. Going from strangers to daters—the whole newness of it—can be sexy and a big turn on.

Romance can come into the picture later. Just get the date first. The supermarket thing can get old. After all, how many melons can you squeeze?

Singles are also getting tired of having their friends and family set them up with "losers" and now want to take the blind date to another level—a level of fantasy and risk. If you play it safe and smart, and use these methods, you have no excuse to be dateless.

Speed Dating FAQs

1 What is Speed Dating?

Speed Dating was created by a Los Angeles rabbi, in the Orthodox Jewish community, as a method for marriage-minded men and women to quickly evaluate potential partners. It's a no-nonsense way of cutting to the chase, in a fun, social environment. It has become so popular that church groups, community centers, clubs, and bars have adopted this dating technique as a way for singles to be forced to talk to each other. It's group matchmaking, with a clever structure to take the pressure off you.

Speed Dating is a quick, exhilarating way to meet lots of singles in one evening. You meet individuals by having brief one-on-one conversations, and then move on to the next. There are companies all over the country that offer this. Speed Dating sessions run from three to ten minutes, and you can meet up to thirty-five people in one night.

2 Why Speed Dating?

This guarantees you "mini" dates. It takes away the need for long, useless babble, uncomfortable moments of silence, and the need to spend money on those you have absolutely no attraction to.

3 How does Speed Dating work?

- An equal number of single men and women gather at a café or bar. The café is filled with "tables for two" and each table is numbered.
- You are given a number or a name tag.
- You will have three to ten minutes, depending on the Speed Dating company running the event. You are also given suggested topics.
- At the end of the time, there is usually a DJ or MC who either rings a bell or plays music to let you know to move on to the next table.
- You are asked to write on a form if you would like to see this person again. (This entails checking a "yes" or "no" box, "hit" or "miss.")
- The men get up from their seats and move to where another woman is waiting to meet them.
- After a certain time, there is a fifteen to twenty minute break, where you can enjoy drinks and appetizers. It's also a great time to flirt with some-one you had your eye on and may not meet because of the number of attendees. Record the names of the people you meet during intermission on your score card.
- If both sides check off the "yes" box, then the organizers let participants know within two days which match had been made and give each side their contact information.

4 **Is three to ten minutes enough time to size up a date?**

Yes. This is not a full-fledged date. As a mini-date, you can really see if there is an attraction there, a chemistry. If you feel nothing in your gut, then three minutes can be too long.

5 **What are the pitfalls of Speed Dating?**

- Companies do not screen the attendees as part of the registration process. Just like on the Internet, you are really meeting a total stranger.
- There is no romance, no flowers, no opening of the door.
- It's all judgmental, and reminds you how important being the perfect weight is. If you weren't planning on knocking off those ten pounds before, you may start now.
- It has a "cattle call" feeling. You must attend these with a strong attitude that you may not meet anyone. Rejection is very difficult to handle, and all the books that tell you "you need to love yourself first," don't know you. There is no cure for rejection, other than *time.*

6 **What is the great advantage of Speed Dating?**

People of all socio-economic backgrounds attend. If you don't like one person, you move on. It pushes you to be bold, daring, and inquisitive. It takes away a lot of B.S. because you will be asking forthright questions out of the box—like "what do you do for a living?"—that you may not normally ask. For women this is critical.

For singles getting back into dating, it's the best way to get out and recharge your batteries. It gets you dressed up and talking again, and it's a great way to practice how to date again. If you're coming here to learn about dating again, the rejection thing may not be as depressing. You may actually welcome it, because after all, you're here as an experiment.

What questions do you need to ask?

- What do you do? (If they say "not working," then you can ask how they support themselves. You only have a few minutes so there's not time to mess around with this key question.)
- What are the three most important things I should know about you?
- What are your hobbies?
- Do you have pets?
- Where did you go to college? (You'll see how educated they are.)
- Have you ever been married? Kids?
- Are you religious?

8 **What are the Speed Dating rules?** (What should you *not* talk about?)

- Don't ask anyone for any contact information. This includes name, email, or business cards.
- You're not allowed to ask anyone if he or she would like another date.
- You're not allowed to ask sexually explicit questions, use lewd language, or say anything threatening or that could be construed as sexual harassment.
- If you meet someone you would like to go out with, you may inform him or her that you'll be putting his or her name on your score card, but don't pressure him or her to do the same for you in return. If he or she is sincerely interested, he or she will put your name down. But a little pressure like this can make a person change his or her mind about putting your name down. You want to date people who want to date you. It's not necessary to play the "salesman."

9 **What should I re-think before checking off "yes" on the scorecard?**

- Aside from a fun conversation, do we really have any common interests?
- Am I choosing this person just because he or she is gorgeous and rich?
- If you take away rich and gorgeous, what really impressed me?

- Am I just checking yes with almost everyone so the chance of getting called is greater?
- Can there be potential for a serious relationship?

After the Speed Dating Event

Be selective. After you receive your matches from the company, narrow down the ones you really want to go out with. You can start with an email and see the response you get. Rejection by email is easier to handle. Email can also create some interesting banter. If you are truly interested in meeting, make sure you say, "I'd like to see you again." You can come right out and say it. This gives the other person time to re-think wanting to see you, and not wasting too much of your time.

Hold back personal information. Still be careful about giving out too much information about where you work, live, or hang out. Unless you really know where this person is from, he or she is still a total stranger.

Pre-screen before committing to meet. Don't invest your hard-earned money and precious time by calling and asking that person out for a date right off the bat. This is a great time to "interview" this person again to see if you will catch a lie. Go through your notes and see if everything is consistent with what you're hearing now.

First say: "I enjoyed meeting you." "Did you have a hard day at work?" "Nice day with the kids?" Bring up subjects that you already talked about.

Then see if he or she remembers you. It's a bad sign if he or she doesn't have a clue as to who you are.

If all seems like it's going well, set up a date. If he or she "hems and haws" too much about how busy he or she is or that he or she isn't sure, and doesn't offer an alternative date, *move on.*

Organize your calendar. If you are in a position where you have a few prospects to go out with, and you're doing the calling, figure out which person you want to meet at Starbucks, and which person you want to take to the Stones concert. Unless you have lots of money to blow, plan wisely.

Remember, people can also be great liars in three minutes. If you proceed with caution, you'll lower your chances of getting hurt.

Is Speed Dating for You?

Although this is an alternative to smoky, crowded bars, are three to ten minutes really going to allow you to size up a person? Speed may be great when it comes time to buying a pair of jeans, or washing your car, but can you really get to know the essence of a person in this arena?

For singles who are not good at small talk, or in situations where they feel pressured and judged, those few minutes of intimidating grilling may blow off any bit of self-esteem or confidence they spent a lifetime building.

This may not be for you.

However, if you approach this with coolness and confidence, and you take it in stride, it could be an interesting way to spend an evening. Best case scenario: walking away with some guaranteed dates.

Worst case scenario: Great stories to tell your friends.

ONLINE DATING

More and more people are turning to online dating as a means to find a date. Years ago, this method seemed desperate, but because of people's busy work schedules and fears, this now seems to be a way to meet people without having to really meet them.

If you are adventurous and willing to understand that this is really a game, and not real, then online dating is for you. It's a *crap shoot*. While you still may meet that special someone, or even a non-special someone, you are literally throwing yourself into a jungle filled with pedophiles, psychos, murderers, freaks, schizophrenics, and swingers.

Unless you don't mind going through this fruit bowl just to pick out the cherries, you may find yourself wasting your time with the pits. Of course, maybe you don't mind pits. The point here is that online dating is filled with weird stuff.

However, there are still people you talk to everyday who meet great people online. This is where you have to be really street smart, savvy, and not gullible.

Online dating is a reflection of the real world, filled with liars, cheaters, and imposters. However, these liars, cheaters, and imposters are the same people who show up at bars, social functions, and your Aunt Martha's wedding reception.

Regardless of how or where you meet someone, dating is always a gamble. The way to win here is not to not do it, but rather to exercise caution and proceed slowly. Hold back on real personal information, especially your address.

You don't want to spend a billion hours corresponding with someone, either by email, or phone, building up all sorts of fantasies about that person, only to find out you're dealing with an eighty-five-year-old pedophile.

Online dating doesn't give you a physical sense of whom you are dealing with. Even if the knowledge of this person is true, that he or she is rich, well versed, and comes from a nice family, if there is no spark or chemistry when you finally meet, I hope you didn't invest too much into this.

For the adventurous type, this can be fun. But you can't treat this meeting as if it were a blind date set up by someone you know.

Top 10 Ways to Protect Yourself

1 Set up a secondary email account.

2 Never give out your last name.

3) Never give out your personal information like address or place of work.

4) Use a cell phone number.

5) When you meet, meet in a public place, and drive yourself.

6) During this meeting, if there is a great inconsistency from all your previous correspondence, run.

7) Keep the meeting short, and now that you've met, for ladies, see how soon you get a call back. If things seem like they are going well, you need to check this person's background out.

8) If you decide during the first meeting to go to another location, go separately.

9) Avoid bike rides, hiking, or drive-in movies. Avoid anything that seems like you wouldn't be able to run if needed.

10) Until the background is checked, avoid home pick-ups.

Find an online service that suits you—there are lots of free ones as well as fee ones. You can do a Google search by typing "online dating" and you'll get a good start there.

According to Netscape.com, Here Are Some of the Top Online Dating Sites:

1 **Date.com**

This online dating service is free to join as a basic member. It provides a whole lot more than personals. The astrology section is fun and guides you through the stars. This was developed by many relationship experts.

2 **Yahoo! Personals**

With some uniquely interesting features, Yahoo! Personals is the second largest of the most popular online personals sites. A search on the Yahoo! Personals site will guide members to click on an individual listing to other broadly similar members, on a profile generated by a new computer program it calls the affinity engine.

3 **Kiss.com**

On average more than six thousand singles join Kiss.com every day, making it the fastest growing online matchmaking and online dating service on the Internet. Kiss.com offers the most comprehensive online matchmaking service facilities and there are always thousands of people online making new friends.

4 **Udate.com**

With private email, and whispers instant messaging, Udate.com is a great way to find new singles. They average thirty people joining each hour, so you should never run short in finding someone to chat with.

5 **FriendFinder.com**

This site has the largest network of online dating sites on the Internet. You can browse through their enormous database of free personals, or chat directly with singles that are logged on.

6 **DreamMates.com**

This site is considered to be one of the largest dating sites in North America, with over 3.5 million members.

7 **Match.com**

This site has grown since 1995 to become of the Internet's most recognized and respected dating brands. The site is well designed and provides many features.

Matchmaking Services

Search terms:

"Dating services"

"Matchmaking services"

"Introduction services"

"Professional matchmaker"

"Upscale"

"Exclusive"

"Elite"

Today's matchmaking market is not like it was in the '50s, when little old ladies sat in their kitchens reading tea leaves and tarot cards. Matchmaking services are everywhere and cost bucks. These are better because at least there is a personal connection, so you can grill the workers about any of the candidates.

Your picture and personal profile are all that the other person can go by, so be as honest as you can.

For those services that offer videotaped interviews, make sure you get to see the video before you're done. You may want to re-do some of it. If you break down crying in the middle of talking about your ex, I'd recommend you re-shoot it.

PERSONAL ADS

Like matchmakers, personal ads have been around for decades. Personal ads are just like online dating, but you don't get to see the picture at first so you are totally relying on the text of the ad. The ad is either true, or a total lie. It's worth taking the risk, but exercise the same caution you would when meeting any other stranger.

With the competition out there, and no photo of yourself, the only thing you have going for you is your ad header. The way it's worded can make or break your chances of having that person respond to your ad.

When you finally sit down to write the ad, it's okay to plagiarize other ads that you've seen. If it works, it works. This isn't college and you don't have to worry about getting kicked out for copying an ad you saw in a magazine ten years ago or yesterday.

With the hundreds of ads out there you need something that sets you apart from the masses. You need catchy phrases that will make people look twice at your ad.

Catchy Ad Headers for Personal Ads or Online Dating
Men Seeking Women:

- I bathe everyday.
- Is this thing like Ebay?
- Willing to lie about how we met.
- Coffee, Chocolate, and Men—some things are just better rich
- Open for convincing
- Very normal
- Write me! I hardly ever bite!
- Been there done that? Me too!
- New beginnings
- Single by circumstance or intent?
- Is there someone out there for me?
- To be continued...
- Looking for sexy & stable—Is that too much to ask?
- Only single ladies need apply! Not the cheating type.
- Hey you...yes you...c'mere...check this out.

Women Seeking Men:

- Warm smile, warm heart
- Do you have my glass slipper?
- I'm looking for normal.
- Going fishing in a different pond
- Cute, Fun, Athletic, and Intelligent?
- I'm the girl next door looking for neighborly love.
- Looking for sexy and stable...Is that too much to ask?
- Cute, Adventurous, and Genuine
- You must be over 5'10" to read this.
- I believe in dragons, good men, and other fantasy creatures.

Radio Station Set Ups

Another wacky way to get a date is calling in to your local radio station. Many of them have their DJ's fix people up on the air. It's a really long shot, but worth the try.

The Whole Photo Thing

Everything in blind dating, from set ups to online, matchmaking to personals, will eventually lead to wanting to see a photo of that person. It is very important that you look like your photo when you meet. You're better off showing a less flattering photo. It's better to hear afterwards how much better you look than your picture. There should be no surprises.

If a picture is worth a thousand words, then how about a thousand responses? Profiles with attractive photos attract up to seven times more responses. Try to use a digital camera. If you can't borrow one, most dating services can scan your picture if you mail it to them.

Twenty Tricks to Make Your Photo Pop

1. If you're not extra lean, keep your shirt on.

2. Don't have an arm slung around someone else's waist.

3. Don't stand in front of a yacht, unless it's yours.

4. Don't squint.

5. Don't show your tattoos.

6. Smile and show your teeth. If you are missing them, get some before you post your photo.

7. Don't wear shades that hide your eyes.

8. Don't make a funny face, unless you want to date Bozo.

9. Use a recent photo. If you're forty, don't use your high school graduation picture (unless you just recently graduated).

10. Crop out the strip joint sign in the background.

11 A joint in one hand and a bottle of beer in the other is not a good idea.

12 Don't use your mug shot. Think of Nick Nolte.

13 A mountain range in the background is nice, but not with your ex, on your honeymoon.

14 Lose the cowboy hat. Bald can be sexy.

15 Cut-off muscle shirts are out, unless you have the muscle to back it up.

16 A parrot on your shoulder, or French kissing your cat, may send out the wrong message.

17 Don't send the picture of you sitting on Santa's lap. Remember the one from the office party? That one.

18 Consider the wall décor behind you. The moose's head may be offensive to vegetarians.

19 The bathrobe pose also doesn't work unless you're in a video with JLo and Ben.

20 Give it your best shot.

However you write your ad, or whatever picture you use, you must set yourself apart from everyone else. When you're writing your ads, use words that are alive, playful, and daring. But don't lie about how you look like Demi Moore, because that will be hard to pull off if you really don't look that way. Eventually you will have to meet these people.

The best way to test your ad is to run it by your friends. Mix your ad with a bunch of others and see what jumps out. You may have to rework your catch phrases.

Why Personal Ads?

1 Personal ads allow you to be gutsy and really spell out what you want.

2 They are anonymous so you can be really specific about what you want.

3 You're apt to get responses from those who have similar interests.

4 There is a mystery to this that makes your dating life far more exciting.

5 Your chances of getting to meet someone exciting increase, because those who respond to personal ads have a little adventurous streak in them as well.

How To Answer Ads

Ads that entice people to respond can get anywhere from ten to three hundred hits. Your response to an ad must show you to be as interesting as the person who wrote the ad. If you want to get noticed, you should come up with clever, catchy ways to respond.

1 **Don't respond right away.** Wait about a week so that by the time you send in your response, your chances of standing out will be greater.

2 **Respond to the ad by using the same type of wording, as the original ad.** In the case of "Straight Guy...seeks..." you may say "Straight Woman, with curves..." You want to show you that you got what they were saying.

3 **If the ad asks for your photo, then send the best picture of yourself.**
   ■ Men—Don't send a picture showing you with a group of buddies, clicking beer cans at a strip joint. Let her find out about that side of you later.
   ■ Ladies—Don't send a picture of you in your business suit. Not sexy, unless your blazer is open showing your teddy underneath. I know you're a successful CEO of a major cosmetics firm, but sitting on your mahogany desk in a slinky black dress is sexier.

- Don't send a head-shot. They look fake.
- Don't send a postage stamp size picture either. Not everyone has 20/20 vision.
- Photos should be happy, sexy, and really look like you. Not cheesy, not trampy, but classy. Profiles that include photos get many more responses.

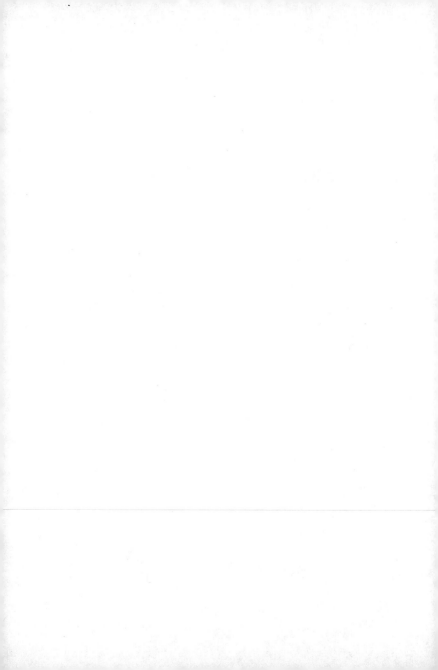

chapter seven:

Making the First Move

Now that you've got yourself a whole new look and a whole new attitude, it's time to get out there. Traditionally it's been men who have had to carry the burden of making the first move, but today, women are also asking men out. The good news is that *men love this!* It takes a whole lot of pressure off them and men find it sexy when a woman "comes on to them."

Top Five Ways to Get Started

1 **Go out with friends.**

There are more ways of scoring dates when you head out with your posse. There's always one friend in the group who will be the "ice breaker" when you find someone you want to meet. This cuts your work in half, and saves you serious effort in making the first move.

2 **Just say "hello."**

A sincere "hello" is all you really need. Singles today are too savvy and hip to go for a pick up line. They've heard it all. Unless it's a flattering, complimentary line, like "I couldn't help but notice your eyes," which works because men truly love complimenting women, and women should be sweet enough to say "thank you."

3 Be an interesting conversationalist.

Once you catch that person's attention you have to keep the conversation going. Keep a few good stories handy. Since most small talk centers on movies, music, and other topics of popular interest, keep an eye on current trends. Watch the news, read magazines, and learn from conversations with other people. Since people also love to talk about themselves, let them talk, while you're the good listener.

4 Keep an open mind.

Don't be too quick to judge someone, unless the chemistry has no way of developing. But if there's something there, give it some time. The other person is nervous too, and may behave in a way that is not really a reflection of who he or she is. You may be dismissing someone too soon. If that person has the looks and the smarts, but sounds like Daffy Duck, that's something you can't change. Unless you can get used to that voice, you may need to move on.

5 Be comfortable with yourself. Or at least pretend to be.

Keep in mind that no matter how much you beat

up on yourself, there are qualities that you have that are desirable. If you're overweight, broke, and have no job, then maybe you're a great musician, chef, or poet. Find that one thing and focus on that. If you don't show a level of comfort with yourself, then it will be hard for another person to get close to you as well. If you hate yourself, it's hard to let another person love you. You will resist others in some way. Find the quality or talent in yourself that you truly love.

COMMON DATING ADVICE MYTHS

Although I hate to knock other dating advice books, there are things that I read in them that I find to be unrealistic and misleading.

When you are out there dating, it's really hard. You always think you are doing and saying the wrong thing. You never really know what the other person is thinking about you and that creates a lot of pressure on you, about how the date is going.

So many of these other books feed you a pack of bullshit that makes me want to rip out all the pages and crayon in them, "What are you talking about?"

Are you really talking to single people, or are you in your comfortable office with your psychology degrees hanging over your mahogany desk, thinking that you know what singles are really going through. If you really know what the 100 million singles are going through, then you wouldn't be telling them the following crap.

Unrealistic Things You Don't Want to Hear

1 **Have confidence.**

Confidence is such an over-rated word. In fact, it's a myth. I hate it when I read, *have confidence!* "You need to be confident and the world will be yours." Oh, yeah. That's easy for you to say, because you're probably married. But confidence isn't easy. In fact, I don't know if it exists. We all have moments of confidence, but deep down, we are always wondering. I don't believe in people having confidence. I believe in people learning how to hide their insecurities, and pretending they are confident.

Even JLo worried about Ben cheating on her at the strip club. No one is ever really confident. Don't make yourself into something you're not. Don't ever think that confidence in the dating world exists. It doesn't.

2 **Get over rejection.**

Another B.S. fact. Rejection is very hard to deal with. No matter how much you try to tell yourself things like "it's the other person," you can't help but personalize it. Whether you're rejected by a person, a job, a friend, or a dog, it hurts. There are those who get over it faster then others. That's probably because they have more confidence (whatever that means)! There are ways of "masking rejection," but

it's hard to get over it. Only two things really help
with rejection:

1. Time

2. Meeting someone new whom you click with

Coping With Rejection

1 **Go into the approach knowing the other person
will say "no."** I know that sounds like a negative way
to start, but if it means that you'll feel better after,
then who cares. It will now be a positive thing for you.

2 **Walk away fast and keep your dignity.** Don't beg.
Being rejected is hard enough. Why make yourself
look and feel like an idiot?

3 **Surround yourself with good people.** Make it a
point to hang out with those who make you feel welcome and who put you in the limelight. As long as
you're the cat's meow amongst your friends, you'll
start feeling it as well.

4 **Re-visit things you used to be great at.** If you used to
play harmonica very well and gave it up, time to take
it up again. Going back to something that you once
excelled at is another way to boost yourself up again.

5 **Keep yourself looking as good as you can.** When you look in the mirror and you see that outdated outfit, that ratty looking haircut, go and get yourself made over a bit. There's nothing like that "new" look to lift your spirits.

However, if it looks like you are being rejected all the time, it could be you. It's time you looked at your approach and your appearance. It takes seconds for the other person to size you up. Learn to size yourself up as well.

The One-Minute Size Up

I know this may sound harsh, but it can take less than a minute for the other person to size you up and be turned off by you.

Here is what they can capture about you in one minute:

- Nasty nails
- Nasty dandruff
- Nasty shoes
- Nasty breath
- Nasty teeth
- Nasty body odor
- Nasty toes
- Nasty sense of fashion
- Nasty pick up line
- Nasty thing about you (for men, *unemployment*, for women, *a gold-digger*)

Take notice of your teeth, your breath, what you're saying. Notice at what point in the approach you lost the other person. Notice the type of person that other person is going for. No matter how much you try to tell yourself to move on, it's natural to still want to know why you were rejected. Just don't get obsessed with it, or you'll become creepy. You don't want to become that.

TIME TO GET STARTED

Now that you've eyeballed the person you'd like to meet, do a few minutes of observing before you make the approach. Look for a ring. I hate it when married people don't wear rings. It really messes it up for the millions of singles out there who already have enough on their minds.

There should be a law for this.

Overcoming Shyness

Shyness initially comes from a lack of confidence, self-esteem, and fear of rejection. I'm constantly reading about women who say they don't like men who are shy because it makes them look wimpy. Not true.

The single women I spoke to found shy men to be humble, refreshing, and sexy. They were more down-to-earth and honest about themselves. Shy men aren't wimpy. They are cute and are usually hiding a virility that makes them better lovers.

However, until you can get over your shyness enough to talk to anyone, there are ways to calm yourself down.

Dealing With Shyness

Talk to the person as if he or she is a friend. If you make them your friend in your mind, you'll start feeling more relaxed.

Be armed with some great things to talk about. As long as someone is talking you'll be distracted from your shyness.

Don't be afraid to reveal that you are a shy person. Shyness can also be misunderstood for being snobby, so you don't want to give off the wrong impression.

FLIRTING

Creating good chemistry starts with *flirting*. Even if you hate it, you need to know something about it. It's part of the whole package.

Eleven Great Flirting Tips

1 **Have attitude.** Be enthusiastic, open, and positive.

2 **Start new topics of "sexy" conversation.** Show you're interested in that person, and don't put all the pressure on them to guide the conversation. Keep the topics light. Nothing too heavy, like terrorism, cancer, or depression. Talk about sexy things, such as first date fantasies, your favorite kind of lingerie, or a dream weekend getaway.

3 **Have fun.** Show you like to go to parties, functions, and travel. Even if you work in the morgue or with terminally ill people, show you have a fun side.

4 **Great props.** Never leave home without a great conversation piece, like an unusual handbag, a foreign newspaper, an interesting book, or a lingerie magazine, because these can make great conversation openers.

5 **Eye contact.** Make eye contact without staring.

6 **Smile.** Show a great smile! It's inviting and draws people to you.

7 **A great laugh.** People love to be around people who have a fun laugh. If you cackle, tone it down, but laughing is addictive.

8 **Cleavage.** A little cleavage goes a long way. That's a woman's cleavage I'm talking about. If you're a man and you thought I meant you, then you're reading the wrong book.

9 **A pickle in your pocket.** Women notice that little bulge. Whether it's your "pickle" or your wallet, anything that bulges from that area will draw attention.

10 **Smell great.** There's nothing sexier than fresh smelling wrists, neck, hair, and breath. The scent of a woman is what a man will remember long after you're gone.

11 **Lick your lips.** This seems to be the one that drives men wild. If a woman licks her lips in a very subtle way during conversation, it's a real turn on. The way she licks her finger is another one. Not all women are comfortable pulling this one off, but it's worth the try.

Opening the Conversation

The hardest part is breaking the ice. The easiest way is to get a third party to do it for you, like a friend, waiter, or bartender. But that won't always be possible.

Women

Although women are taught to be coy and shy, men today like intelligent, self-assured women. However, there is still a fine line here. Women have to be very careful how they use their knowledge to not come across too bold. There's a real talent in learning how to balance this. Learn it. It can make or break your social life.

Men

Women pick up on the vibe that you want to "bang" them before the main course arrives. As flattering as that may be, it's wise to lay low until you get the signal from her.

This should reflect on your initial approach. No matter how much cleavage she exhibits, you are still better off noticing her "mind." Making your first words to her "Is this seat taken?" is a better choice than "Great knockers lady. Can I sit here?"

Three Ways to Get Her to Talk to You

1. **Don't be sexual with her off the top.** Flatter her in a nice way, like "you've got a great smile." It may sound old and cliché, but it still works.

2. **Ask her about herself.** "How's your day going so far?" This is a great question because if serves two purposes. First, it makes her feel comfortable, and secondly, it's a great way to judge to see if you even want to proceed. If her answer is bizarre, like "Not so good. I'm just over a divorce and I'm planning on killing my ex," you may want to move on. If her response is playful, like "Great day. Just bought lingerie at Victoria's Secret," then you may want to proceed.

3. **Be a good listener.** If she blabs too much without once asking about you, then that's a red flag. If you have a natural chemistry, you're on your way.

Five Ice Breakers to Get the Conversation Going

1. **Notice what's around you.** If she's looking at travel brochures, talk about that. If he's wearing a nice tie, compliment it. However, *keep it positive.* If there's a crying baby near you, don't say "I hate these little brats."

2. **Show generosity.** "Can I get you another cup of coffee?"

3. **Compliments.** Don't gush, but a couple of compliments work.

4. **Movies, books, people in the news.** If there's nothing back, change topics. If there is still nothing, change tables.

5. **Things that interest you.** See if the other person likes the things that you do. You may strike a chord when you bring up how you just tried bungee jumping for the first time, and the other person has always wanted to. Or how much you love walking in the rain. That person may like that as well. You can really judge another person's interests by talking about your own.

Conversation Impressions

DOs

1 **Maintain good eye contact.** Staring at the cocktail waitress shows you're not interested in the person you're talking to, unless it is the cocktail waitress you want to go out with.

2 **Have good body posture.** If you keep slouching, and look sleepy, you'll give off the wrong vibe.

3 **Know the person's name and remember it.** It's embarrassing when you're talking to someone for a half-hour, and he's told you his name three times and you still can't remember it. It's really embarrassing when you finally ask him to spell his name so you can get it right, and he says, "J-I-M."

4 **Talk about food, travel, music, or plays, and see what sparks interest in the other person.** If you talk about something and you get no feedback, you need to find something else to talk about. It's boring to listen to a guy go on and on about some sporting event when you know nothing about it.

5 **Hobbies are fun to talk about,** especially if they're unique, like collecting salt and pepper shakers or

building model airplanes. You can learn a lot about the other person from a hobby alone, and that may determine if you even want to continue with this conversation. If you find out this person collects dead rats, or discarded toilet seats, you may want to move on.

6 **Ask what the other person does for a living.** Other books tell you to avoid this because if the person has a weird job or no job at all, you may be putting them on the spot. You need to know what the other person does for work, because you don't have time to waste and have every right to want to know.

DON'Ts

1 **Don't begin every sentence with "I".**

2 **Don't tell offensive jokes.**

3 **Don't talk about money. Unless you have it, and even then, keep it low key.**

4 **Don't talk about how much you hate your job.**

5 **Don't take over the whole conversation so the other person can't get a word in.**

6 **Don't talk politics, unless you know you share the same parties.**

7 **Don't ask what people own unless they volunteer it.** Not everyone wants to talk about the yacht or shopping plaza he or she owns because he or she will think you're a gold digger. You also may come across as a bragger.

8 **Don't talk about your ex.** The other person really couldn't care less. If you need to get it off your chest, call a friend.

9 **Don't whine about how you never meet anyone decent and how your social life sucks.** You may scare that person off because you'll sound like a complaining loser.

10 **Don't volunteer personal information about yourself** like "I'm broke," "I'm being evicted," "I'm in recovery for gambling," "My father's a pimp," "My mother's cheating on my dad."

11 **Don't talk about things that you don't like about yourself,** like how much you hate your fat ass, your large forehead, and your big feet. The other person most likely wouldn't have noticed that, until now that you've brought it up.

12 **Don't talk about your nasty habits,** like biting your nails until they bleed, or grinding your teeth.

Keep it light. You don't want to load the other person with so much negativity about yourself that he or she runs. The other person will be more intrigued to get to know you better if you don't volunteer your whole life story.

After you've had some conversation, it's time to come right out and ask if it's all right to get together again. Don't play games here. If you truly want to see that person again, show it. If you really don't want to get together, don't. Time is precious. Don't waste it on the wrong person. After you made the first offer and there is no response, give it up. No one wants a stalker. This playing hard to get stuff doesn't work anymore.

Now that you have the number, how long do you wait to make the call?

1 to 2 days.

That's it. Contrary to what people say about "playing the field," "not showing you're desperate," or "keeping them guessing." If you took the number and *sincerely* want to meet up with this person again, *call the next day!!!* Notice how I emphasized "sincerely." That is such an important word in dating because:

1. If you're truly sincere about getting together, then why wait? You're going by what you want to do, which means you're being true to your feelings. If the other

person doesn't like that, then the heck with him or her. If he or she wants to play games, then let him or her play games, but not on your time.

2. If you're *not* sincere, then it doesn't matter how long you wait to call. To call when you're not sincere is only teasing the other person, and that makes you out to be the bad guy.

If you really don't want to call, then don't say you'll call. *Don't mislead anyone.*

If you say you're going to call and you want to get together, then *make the call.*

chapter eight:

Making the Call

THE FIRST PHONE CALL

Now that you're making the first call, it doesn't mean you have to make a date.

All this means is that you're interested in exploring this person further to see if you still want to continue with your plans. Remember the "sincerity" word? Only make the date if, after the phone conversation, you still want to proceed further. Don't make a date out of obligation. The other person will get over it, and why torture yourself?

The reason you shouldn't feel that you have to lock in a date in the initial call is because things can happen on the phone that turn you off and make you feel differently about this person.

Phone Call Etiquette: Tips That Can Make or Break the Date

To Leave or Not to Leave a Message?

1 If they're not home, leave one message.

2 If you have their work number, leave one message.

3 If you have their cell phone number, leave one message.

4 That totals about three messages. If you don't hear back, wait a week, leave one more message on one phone line only.

5 If you left a message with another person, that counts as an answering machine message.

6 If there was no work or cell phone message left, then the calling back one more time rule still applies. After that, give it up.

7 If he or she hasn't called you back, he or she is not interested.

8 Don't keep calling. It's annoying and weird.

9 Even if the other person teased you to the point that you were naming your children together, the point here is that for whatever reason, he or she didn't call you back.

The Actual Call...What If?

1 **What if he or she doesn't remember who I am?**
   Introduce yourself and remind them of how you

met. See if he or she remembers. If so, that's a good sign. If not, you have some more work ahead of you.

2 What if he or she still doesn't remember?

Go into further detail about things that you talked about. If he or she still doesn't remember, laugh about it and see if he or she will see you anyway. If so, then your charm and personality on the phone impressed him or her.

3 What if I really want to meet his or her roommate?

Don't be a B.S. artist. If you called to set a date, and you enjoyed the conversation, and there are no major red flags, then set the date. It's very misleading to talk on the phone with someone for a half hour, only to find out he really wants to date your mother. Be truthful about why you're calling. If the call is really about meeting a cousin who is VP of a company you just sent a resume to, say so.

4 What if the only time I can call is during work hours?

Be courteous about where you are calling. If it's at work, then ask off the top, "Is this a good time to talk?" Even if the answer is "yes," keep the call to about five minutes, state your business, and call later at a more convenient place.

5 **What if I call and the timing isn't right?**

Watch out for the time that you call. Before 9 A.M. or after 10 P.M. aren't good times. Timing is so important in getting the other person excited that you called. You'll hear it in the voice on the other end. If he or she is distracted, this may not have been a good time. Ask when it would be better to call back. If he or she hems and haws, don't call back. If he or she gives you a definite time, then stick to it. You don't want to look flaky.

6 **What if two days have passed, and I'm feeling depressed?**

Don't call if you're in a lousy mood. The other person will pick up your tone and enthusiasm. It's hard to hide a sullen voice, unless you're a great actor. It will also make a bad impression. It's better to wait a few days longer, get your spirits up, and then call. It's not fair to you or the other person. However, keep one thing in mind. Your spirits may be lifted if you make the call and have a nice date to look forward to.

7 **What if I want to make a date, and I hear my potential date yelling and screaming at whomever in the background and acting all loony?**

I'd hold off on making a date. That's a red flag. Loony is hard to hide, unless you're loony too, and have met your match. We're all really loony, but there has to be some sort of a sense of control at first. Anyone who feels so free to behave like that on an initial call has no sense of what he or she is doing, which is a big sign of the way they handle other things in life. Just remember, you may be the recipient of these outbursts one day, so run while you can.

8 **What if I make the call, we talk for two hours, I ask to set a date, and he or she says "No"?**

As humiliating as that is, try to see if the "no" comes from a place of that other person being really scared because he or she just got out of a bad relationship, or is moving and doesn't want to start anything. Snoop around for a reason. There are definite signs during the conversation that will let you know.

For example: If during the call a woman asks, "What do you do?" and you say "Nothing, really...I'm trying to find myself," don't blame her for saying no. That is a major red flag for a woman, and she is saving you time and money by not going out with you. It's not what she wants.

Another example: If during the call a man asks a woman if she's ever been married, or has kids, and she says she's going through a messy divorce, is about to lose her house, and can't feed her five kids, then the man most likely won't want the date. These are things that really scare off the other person. No one wants to get in the middle of a messy domestic situation.

Understand what "no" is. Then again, "no" can just be as simple as "no" without any sense of why.

That's part of the dating game. Call someone else.

9 **What if I called twice and left messages with someone else, but I still haven't heard back?**

Call one more time. If you left the message with a kid, it's highly likely that they didn't pass along your message. Young kids can't be relied on to relay a message. If the person you left the message with answers again, don't be afraid to ask nicely if he or she told so and so you called. It's a polite reminder and lets you know where you stand. If he or she insists your message was forwarded, then it's time to move on. If he or she calls, fine, but if not, more than three messages is too much. You don't want to harass anyone.

10 **What if a man answers?**

If you're a man yourself and a man answers, it might be nice to know who that person is. If you're a heterosexual and dating the opposite sex is important to you, then explore who this person is. If you're a woman and a man is answering your phone, and it's not your son, father, or brother, then the caller has the right to know who it is. Nobody wants to start off dating someone who still has her ex living with her.

11 What if the other person only suggests a coffee date? What's that about?

Don't feel that you're not worthy of an in-depth date if it's just coffee. Coffee dates can lead to marriage. Coffee dates tell me that the other person is practical. Coffee dates can be sexy because they are a tease to the real thing. Coffee dates are a relief. If there's no chemistry, then you're off the hook after you swoosh down you last gulp and bolt out of there before your foam even melts. However, whoever asked for this coffee date, *must pay for the coffee* and the Danish that goes with it. If he or she doesn't, get out fast.

12 What if he or she won't give me an address to pick him or her up for the date?

If this is a blind date, women should be cautious of having anyone they really don't know pick them up from their home. Men should be respectful of this. Between stalkers, rapists, psychos, and weirdos, women should never put themselves in a vulnerable situation. Women should never feel pressured into giving out their address, no matter how pushy the man is about this. If a woman feels that the man is being too hardheaded about meeting her in a neutral public place, then she should reconsider the date.

13 What if he asks me how I look in a bikini?

This question is loaded with lots of "reading in between the lines" stuff. It's a golden moment to see if you even want to date this person. If this question is coming from a man over the age of thirty, to a woman over the age of twenty-five, it's a *red flag*. If you truly don't look good in a bikini, and that seems to be his priority, then dump him.

If you look good in a bikini, and that is his priority, then dump him anyway. Very few women can sustain looking good in a bikini no matter what. This is a question that has too much baggage attached to it.

14 What if he asks what kind of lingerie I like?

This is a great question. It's sexy, and can fit all types of women. Women of all shapes and sizes can look sexy in the right lingerie. This is a man who is adventurous, and is not afraid to show it.

15 What if he or she never calls?

Don't hang on to one person calling you. With one hundred million single people out there, there is someone out there wanting to call you.

Now that you've decided to make the call, know why you're calling. If you're calling to *make a date*, make sure you do that (unless you change your mind during the conversation). If you're calling just to

talk, and not set a date, *don't call*. If you need someone to talk to, call a shrink.

As difficult as the first call is, you'll feel better
once you start talking to the other person. This will
validate whether or not this person is still interested
in you. If he or she is vague, cold, and indifferent on
the phone, cut the call, and move on. Sometimes
people give off one vibe when you see them, and
another when you make the call. Your gut should tell
you whether this person is happy you're calling. If you
don't feel that, but are still not sure, cut to the chase
and ask if he or she wants to get together. Sometimes
the other person too shy to show excitement. The
only way to be sure if he or she interested is if he or
she agrees to see you.

Setting Up the Date

Assuming the conversation is going great, there are no
obvious red flags, and the phone chemistry is starting to
click, it's time to set the date. Close the deal.

Here Are Some Quick Tips to Have Ready at Your Fingertips for Setting Up the Date.

1 **Listen to what the other person likes.** Don't be
selfish. If you're told that this person doesn't like
hiking, don't suggest a rough sport. Ask him or her
first what he or she likes. If he or she asks you to

decide, then don't be wishy-washy. Have a list of fun things to do. The same goes for food. If the other person is a vegetarian, then besides that being a possible red flag, don't offer to go a pig roast.

2 **If you can't make it this weekend, then offer alternatives.** If you don't suggest a better time to meet, then you probably don't want this date. But if you do, be helpful with what is good for you. It's really annoying to try to make a date with someone who won't offer feedback. It's so annoying that I would suggest that if you are the recipient of this, you may want to make a quick decision on the spot and reconsider if you even want to continue making plans for a date. You really want to make a date with someone who is equally interested in the date as you are.

3 **Be clear with what you are planning.** If you're planning a formal night out, then it can be embarrassing if your date shows up in khakis. If it's a surprise kind of date, tell the person to pack two kinds of clothing— one for casual and one for dressy.

4 **Don't make it inconvenient for the other person to meet you.** If you live on totally opposite sides of town, meet halfway. The really nice thing would be for the man to meet 80 percent of the way. The not nice thing would be for the woman to expect the man to meet her

100 percent of the way. It's nice for him to offer, but she should still say she'll meet 20 percent of the way.

HOW TO INCREASE YOUR SEX APPEAL OVER THE PHONE

Men love a woman's voice. Her inflections, pauses, and responses can give him a warm feeling before the date even starts.

Ten Proven Ways Women Can Turn Men On Over the Phone

1 **Be a good listener.** Don't interrupt.

2 **Ask questions about him.**

3 **Ask questions about what turns him on.** Just keep it vague and not sexual. If you ask him what size breasts he prefers, that may make him uncomfortable. Keep it light. For example, "What's your favorite color on a woman?" "Do you like cooking?" "What foods turn you on?" These lead to sexy thoughts. That's all you're trying to do here—keep his imagination pumping. That's a turn on for men.

4 **Even if he says he wants your honest opinion about something, lie.** He really doesn't want to know that

he messed up at work, and shouldn't have told his boss to take a hike. Just listen and sympathize.

5 **Speak softly.** Your CB radio truck driver voice is best left at the job.

6 **If you have a "cackle" type laugh, try to tone it down.** Besides being annoying, it's unfeminine.

7 **In a subtle way, talk about how you love lingerie.** The word "lingerie" is enough to get him hot. Tell him you're wearing some now.

8 **Bring up how you love to cook for your man.** This brings out a "motherly" nurturing quality in you, and in some sick way, men love that. As much as they may have conflict with their mothers, they seek those qualities in the women they date.

9 **In a subtle way, talk about how you love giving your man a nice massage.** You don't have to make it sound like you're an expert, but you can be leading and say things like "I love to relax in front of the TV and give my date a neck massage."

10 **When he asks what you look like, only talk about your good points.** You can tell him how people compliment you on your great eyes and great smile, how

you look great in jeans and a tank top, or how soft your skin is. A man will blow that image up ten times more in his head. That's a real turn on for him.

Two Things Proven to Turn On a Woman Over the Phone

1. **A man with a sizable income.** Women want a man who has ambition, drive, goals, a good job, or a trust fund. They want to know right off the top that they don't have to support him. It's hard enough for a woman to cut it as it is. Even if she has money, there's something about having to take care of a man financially that makes him look weak. Women like strength, no matter how strong she is.

2. **A man who calls.** Women will stay up all night waiting for the call. It's sick, subservient, and desperate. Even if they go out, they run back to see if he called. If you say you're going to call, call. That in itself is a turn on for women. If you call too late, you'll have to make up for it somehow.

How to Turn a Man Off During the Phone Call

1. **Mention anything about how you're still hung up over your ex.** Even if you're over him, his name alone is a turn off. Men don't like to hear names.

2 **Don't mention how much you hate your weight, big nose, or yellow teeth.** Don't mention anything negative about yourself. Remember, it's over the phone. A man's imagination can put out some weird images over the phone wires.

3 **Don't talk about first date sexual hang ups,** like how you never kiss on a first date. This makes you sound rigid, frigid, and men are turned off by anything that ends with the letters "igid."

4 **Don't be the therapist.** Don't remind him of how wrong he is. He probably knows that. He doesn't want to hear it from you. Just listen.

5 **Don't mention how much you hate dating.** Don't tell him how you look at dating like going out with a friend first, then whatever happens, happens. Men hate the "friend" word. They find it insulting. Even if you think this way, keep it to yourself.

6 **Keep nasty habits from creeping into the phone line.** If you just had a beer, don't belch. Belching is not sexy. If you like to grind your teeth, cover the phone. Anything that's distracting, like a loud annoying habit, should be hidden.

7 **Don't stuff your face while talking on the phone.**
The chomping of an apple, potato chips, or anything
other than a liquid, is magnified a thousand times
more on the other end.

8 **Don't engage in detailed conversation while intox-
icated.** You'll regret what you say—if you remember
what you said the next day. A little booze to ease your
nerves is always fine, but total inebriation is a turn
off. Men like "dirty" talk—but not that dirty.

9 **Don't yap away without coming up for breath.** Men
have a short attention span. While you're yapping
away for twenty minutes about your decorating plans
for your new bathroom, he's already dialing the next
person.

10 **Don't sound too smart.** Although men like intelligent girls, if you show it all off at the beginning, he'll
feel intimidated. Save your knowledge about how
you're the one who came up with the mathematical
equation that gets astronauts to Mars. It will give you
something to talk about on the date.

DEALING WITH "NO"

You've just spent an hour talking to the other person about
all your likes, and listening to his or hers. Now it's time to
set the date and you get a flat "no." Do you call back? *No.*

144 ■ dating confidential

It goes back to an old saying "What part of no don't you understand?" No is no. No is not maybe. No is not "I'm just messing with your head." No is not yes. No is no.

No matter how much you go over the call in your head, I promise you there are hints and signs along the way that should let you know that a *no* is coming.

- She tells you she's not over her ex.
- He tells you he's not ready to date because of other emotional issues.
- She tells you she's moving.
- He tells you he's gay, bi, or transgendered.
- She tells you she is looking for a blonde and you're a redhead.

...or it could be something you said.

...or you'll just never really know.

Somewhere in there is the reason. If you can't figure it out, "no" is still "no." And no matter why it's "no," you don't call back to ask why. You'll never get the real answer. Would you give an honest answer? *No*.

No person in his or her right mind would give an honest answer. Why? He or she doesn't owe you anything. People aren't comfortable when they have to be totally honest. Especially when it comes to telling a person why "no" is "no." It sucks, it may not be the most decent thing, but you can't fight human nature. Being truthful as to why a "no" is a "no" has always been the hardest thing for people to confront.

So how do you deal with "no"? You can't deal with it. There's nothing to deal with because you have no control over what's going on in the other person's mind. You can't make this person go out with you unless you break laws. That's not going to do you any good while you serve time in prison. Being rejected is something we have to program ourselves to deal with, because it's coming in anything we do. Whether it's dating, work, or with friends, life is filled with rejections. It's hard to deal with. That's why you shouldn't have to deal with it. You should just find something else to focus on, and you'll feel better.

The phone call is the prelude of what's to come. You want to make the other person excited about meeting you and going out. You want to be excited as well. This is part of the whole excitement about dating. The phone call can make or break the way people look at you, before even seeing you. If you blow it on the phone, it's hard to make up for it. Looks and money do help, but you better be really good looking and be really rich, if you think you can get away with any kind of behavior on the phone.

Don't be a tease. If you come across as the sexpot on the phone, and practically had phone sex, don't show up on the date like a real prude. Don't make yourself out to be one way over the phone and another in person. Being a tease is misleading, totally misrepresents who you are, and is a really shitty way to be.

chapter nine:

Things to Do on a First Date

The first date is really about getting to know if you have any chemistry or compatibility. It's not about going out with someone just so you have an ear to spew out your whole life story too. If you had great conversation, but no *fun*, because you or your date is too intense or your lives are too problematic, then you may want to think twice before going out again.

IF DATING IS NO FUN, WHY DO IT?

I've heard too many times about two people from broken, desperate backgrounds who hook up for the sole reason that they can relate to each other's problems. Every soul needs to find a balance. If the person you're with doesn't offer that balance, then what kind of life are you setting up for yourself?

One young man recently told me how his mother is suffering from cancer, eviction, no money, and how his date is getting over cancer herself, a drug problem, molestation, and is living in the garage of her parole officer. He says that their whole date was talking about their problems. When I asked him if he had any fun, he said, "Who can have fun with all these problems?" He was only twenty-three years old.

The point here is that he should be with someone who can show him a good time, how to have fun. This poor young girl should also be with someone who can show her the *fun side* of life. With all the problems people have, it is important in dating to find your fun side.

Don't settle because you feel this is the kind of person who can relate to you. If a relationship/friendship is solely based on sharing tragic events, then when things lighten up for one and not the other, you may not be as compatible as you had thought.

That's why what you choose to do on a first date is so important. Everyone experiences problems, sorrow, and loss. That's just the reality of life. The first date should be an escape from all your suffering. Many of you may feel that this would be starting the date on a false note, but that's not true. It might be true if you were starting a *relationship* that way. That's a whole different set of rules. Dating rules should not be mistaken for relationship rules.

True, dating can lead to a relationship, but for the most part, dating is just going out with someone to see if you click. Some people are so lucky that they click without ever having to date. There's a magic and instant attraction from the second they meet. For others, that may happen on the fifth date, or never at all. It's so important to recognize when the person you're dating really wants to date you too. It can't be one sided. If you're always wondering if he or she will call, then it's not there. He or she just isn't into you. People who *are* into you will make the call or return the call.

It works at a different pace for everyone.

This is why we have so many dating books, dating advice columnists, and on-line dating services. Dating itself is difficult because it's a social concept totally based on chemistry and reading the other person. Very few people have this kind of insight to themselves, let alone others.

No matter how smart, rich, or successful you may be, when it comes to matters of the heart, it's hard to ever really be sure. It's only by getting out there, as often as you can, that you will truly start developing a sense of what works for you. The way you acted on a date at age twenty may be different from how you act on a date at age twenty-five. You look back and see how you did things. Why she or he didn't return your call. You look back and go over in your head, over and over again, the fact that you didn't tip the waitress, that your car was a mess, or that you were out of work. Today at age twenty-five, for a guy, maybe you're getting the babes because you now have a great job; for ladies, you've lost that college weight, and have some spending money for a new look.

Who Pays for What

Here it is in a nutshell:

If the man asks the woman out, he pays for the date. *The whole date.*

If the woman asks the man out, she pays just for the dinner part, or the tickets part. If there are more things in the date, like food, parking, drinks, or tips, the man pays for them. It may not sound like an even balance, but men should really be paying. Even if she asks you out, it's still better for the man to pay. If she's already bought tickets to something, then you don't have to pay for something she's already bought, but the man should definitely pay for the rest of the date. You may think this rule isn't fair, but it goes hand in hand with men wanting a woman with great looks—women want men who have money and who will pay for the date. Don't listen to your modern generation X kids or siblings who tell you the contrary. The man pays.

The woman should also not be a pig and order four appetizers, five drinks, and the most expensive thing on the menu. She should order modestly. If it looks like her date has been spending a lot of money on her, then she shouldn't take advantage of him and keep ordering more things. It wouldn't hurt for her to offer to buy him a coffee afterwards, if she can afford it.

I know women who, during the date, realize the guy is a real asshole and purposely start ordering whatever they want. Nothing is wrong with this. If you're with a guy who is pushing to have sex with you right away, who brags about all the women he's "banged," and who has the bucks to blow—why not? At the end of night, he'll get what he deserves and you'll get to share some stories with your friends the next day.

It may sound spiteful, evil, and appalling that I would endorse such behavior, but after talking to hundreds of people over ten years, I believe that sometimes a woman's got to do what she's got to do.

These are things in life that haven't changed and never will. It's a deep part of our genetic make up. It's like a good black cocktail dress. Something things never go out of style.

Top Eight Reasons Why Things Go Bad on a Date

1 **You find out the other person lied about who they are.** He isn't really a lawyer, but a law student who has failed at every attempt at the bar, and is now tending to a different bar—mixing cocktails.

2 **She has more kids than you knew about.** You didn't know until the date that this woman has three kids who live with her, and another three in college. This should have been disclosed over the phone. No one likes surprises.

3 **The person arrived late—really late.** Not a few minutes, but hours, and didn't call. That's enough to get you in a really bad mood. By the time your inconsiderate date arrives you've already bad-mouthed him to your entire block and friends in different cities. You are so disgusted with this person that you don't even want to go out with him. The person has to be really

good looking or rich (or have a great excuse, like being abducted and locked in the car trunk on the way to the date) to bail out of this one.

4 **Weird stuff you find out.** You find out this person likes threesomes, drugs, and orgies, but none of this behavior was implied on the phone. Unless you're into this stuff, it's weird.

5 **Rude behavior.** Things go really bad on dates when you see your date behaving badly to the waiter or ex she just bumped into. Jeckle and Hyde personalities can really scare another person off. For example, if her demeanor with you is calm and relaxed and then the waiter brings the burger with onions on it and your date goes completely ballistic, that's a red flag. You know it'll be you eventually.

6 **Emotional dysfunction.** Yes, this could be any of us, but some of us can hide it better than others. If your date tells you about his wacky phobias, like the fear of climbing stairs, or sleeping with the sound of car horns honking, then you better wake up to this. Usually this is just the tip of an iceberg of many other wacky dysfunctions.

7 **No gentlemanly protocol.** If the man doesn't open doors, or walks way ahead of you, or stares at the wait-

ress, or talks on his cell phone all night, then this can ruin a date.

8 **Sex, sex, sex.** If one person wants it and the other doesn't, and the one who wants it is really pushy, obnoxious, and freaky about it, then this can ruin the date. Nothing is wrong with a man asking for it, or wanting it. It's the way men are. Women should wake up to this reality, but in a civilized world, it has to be a two-way street.

Seven Important Things You Need to Know Before Going Out

1 **Make sure you have reservations, or the tickets with you before you venture out.** Another big *Love Connection* complaint was how nothing was organized or planned. It's pretty annoying to drive two hours so you can go horseback riding, only to find out the stable shut down years ago.

However, what I did find out was that if the chemistry was there, it didn't matter. Couples who clicked didn't care where they were. They could be sitting in a parking lot playing the geography game. This was an exception. Not everyone is this lucky. So for the most part, try and be a little organized. The worst thing is being stuck with someone you don't know, don't really like, and not have anything to do.

2 **Find out what the other person likes.** The date can be doomed if you go to the home and garden show and your date is totally bored by this.

3 **Know what things cost.** It's embarrassing when you get the check or have to buy tickets for something only to find out you don't have enough money on you.

4 **Know where you're going.** Driving in circles to find something may not only make you late but will piss off your date.

5 **Don't do errands with your date on the way to wherever you're going.** It's inconsiderate and selfish. Too often I heard how, before it even got going, the date was doomed because of errands. Pick up your dry cleaning or return your late videotapes on your own time.

6 **Know the name of the person you're going out with!!!!!**

7 **Say thank you at the end of the date.** Even if the date sucked, end it on a classy note.

Forty Fun Places to Go or
Fun Things to Do on a Date

1 **Dinner.** Dinner can be fun anywhere. If you are in a fun mood, which is what you should be on a date, then even going to McDonald's can be fun.

2 **Plays.** Pick one that's not tragic. Remember, you want to laugh and have fun.

3 **Sports event.** As long as you know your date loves sports, whether it's a hockey game, tennis match, or monster trucks, this is a real hoot.

4 **Concert.** Confirm with your date that they like this type of concert. Not everyone is into Yani or mosh pits.

5 **Dancing.** Dancing is fun, sexy, and wild, just the way a date should be.

6 **Comedy or magic club.** You can find lots of laughs and get to know if your senses of humor are compatible. These places usually have a two-drink minimum. Soda counts as one drink, but you'll pay big-time for it.

7 **The zoo.** This can be great if you're into animals. There are romantic paths to walk, and lots of time to talk.

8 **Art galleries.** If you know a lot about art but your date doesn't, be careful about showing off your knowledge. This can be a great place to get conversation going and have some laughs at the same time.

9 **Museum.** They can be exciting if you're into history.

10 **Coffee house.** This is a great place to talk, relax, and kick back.

11 **Cocktails.** A great way to start a date is with cocktails, to loosen up and see if you want to continue with the date. Just remember, don't get drunk!!!

12 **Brunch.** Sundays are a great time to meet someone without losing a Saturday night.

13 **County fair.** You can play games, hear music, and eat food.

14 **Beer or candy factory tour.** The Food Network has brought us backstage to some of America's most interesting tours. Not only are these places a barrel of fun, the free samples aren't so bad either.

15 **Health spa.** These places cost some bucks but if you can afford it, what a great way to get to know each other. There's nothing like a mud bath to break the ice.

16 **Rodeo.** If you love to holler and scream, this is the place.

17 **Dinner cruise.** This is one of the most romantic dates.

18 **Wine tasting.** These are sexy, fun, and a great way to get a nice buzz. There are lots of other people to interact with as well to take the edge off of first date jitters.

19 **Hot air balloon ride.** A very romantic, daring, thrilling date where you both get to be a little nuts.

20 **Psychic or tarot card reading.** If you don't believe in this stuff, it's a fun way to poke fun at what they're saying. If you do believe in it, make sure you tell the reader you're on your first date so she can tailor the reading appropriately.

21 **Hot tubbing.** This was popular among *Love Connection* daters. If you're not too shy to put on a bathing suit, then it's a really sexy way to start the date.

22 **Amusement park.** These are lots of fun, and can be romantic (remember the movie *Big*?). Don't go on the roller coaster if you think you might throw up.

23 **Picnic.** Try a picnic on your living room floor, especially when it's snowing or raining outside. Light

some candles, add some wine, great music, and a romantic movie, and the night is yours.

24 **Book signing.** If you're interested in the topic, this can be a great date, and you'll look smart for suggesting it.

25 **Horse racing.** It's fun to place a small bet and cheer for your horse. Watch out for signs of gambling addiction, though.

26 **Flea market.** Take a casual stroll up and down the aisles and pick up a little memento or two.

27 **Cook dinner for your date.** Even if you cater it, or have your mother cook it, it's a nice, relaxed way to get to know each other. (Be sure to clean out your medicine cabinet. Your date will snoop.)

28 **Rent a limo and be chauffeured around town.** Check out the tourist sights.

29 **Go to a function at church or synagogue.** This is especially good if you're both of the same faith. Otherwise, it could be dicey.

30 **Karaoke.** Okay, this is not for the shy, but you can have a blast.

31 **Bingo.** A fun, organized activity that gives you something to focus on besides being nervous.

32 **Play a complete game of Monopoly.** It may take forever, but you'll really get to know each other.

33 **Have wacky games ready to play,** from jump rope to Twister to a hula-hoop.

34 **Leave your car at home, if possible, and walk to your destination.** You'll have a nice relaxed time and plenty of chances to talk.

35 **Dine at a truck stop.** The good ones have really extensive menus with down-home cooking. Be sure to have pie. It's worth the drive.

36 **Dog or cat show.** Whether you have a pet or not, it can be great fun to check out the animals. Not a good idea if one of you is allergic.

37 **Rent a foreign film with English subtitles.** This can make for sophisticated conversation.

38 **Solve a Rubik's cube.** This is for the brainy ones— make sure your date is up for it.

39 **Find a Greek or Moroccan restaurant with belly**

dancers. They usually put on a great show, and the atmosphere is lively.

40 **Buy a model car or airplane and built it.** It sounds like child's play, but it's a relaxing activity that you can both enjoy. Coloring books and crayons are also great fun.

Butt-Watching Dates

Maybe it's insane to put this in its own category, but admit it—people truly are attracted to each other's butts. The physical attribute I heard described most commonly at *Love Connection* were people's dates' big butts. It seemed to boil down to how good someone looked in a pair of jeans.

So if a major part of the whole sex appeal process is how good your ass looks in a pair of jeans, why fight it? Let's join it.

Here are some great date ideas for checking out each other's butts:

- Bowling
- Pool halls
- Salsa dancing
- Rock climbing
- Horseback riding
- Roller skating
- Hiking
- Bicycling

- Waxing your car
- Walking up stairs

Fifty Unusual, Weird or Wacky Dates

During my survey, I asked singles what some of their more unusual first dates were. These are great ideas because they're imaginative and if your date turns out to be a dud, hopefully where you're at on the date will make up for it.

Getting to know another person can put a lot of pressure on you. If you pick something fun that you enjoy it will ease some of that tension while you experience new things.

1. Party crash in a fancy hotel.

2. Wild museum exhibit.

3. Drive-through restaurant; serve at home with champagne.

4. Get a bunch of magazines, go to a bar, and do all the relationship quizzes together.

5. Go sky diving.

6. Create your own contest, like Oreo stacking or building a house of cards, and see who wins. The loser has to buy dinner.

7 Bake a cake for a friend.

8 Take a cooking class.

9 Go restaurant hopping. Start at one place for the appetizer, go to another for the main course, and another for dessert.

10 Try an oyster bar or sushi bar.

11 Stroll through a flower market.

12 Go on a train or subway ride. Go to places and stations that are new for both of you.

13 Take a ceramics class and make your own pottery.

14 Shoot some hoops at a high school gym.

15 Dress formally and go to a 5-star restaurant.

16 For city folks, take a ride to the country and find local shops to walk around in.

17 Patronize a rowdy saloon.

18 Try an ethnic food that neither of you have ever eaten before

19 Visit an all-night restaurant in the middle of the night.

20 Dine on foods that you loved as a kid, from Captain Crunch cereal to Yoohoo drinks.

21 Host an indoor beach party, with volleyball and beach balls.

22 Throw a party to honor an historical figure.

23 Make candy apples.

24 Gather up great classic comedy recordings, from George Carlin to Chris Rock, sit on the floor, laugh, and get cozy.

25 Spend a day on a farm. If you already live on a farm, try a day in the city.

26 Watch the sunrise.

27 Share the fantasy of how you would spend a million dollars in a week.

28 Learn how to juggle.

29 Rent a tandem bike.

30 Make a pizza.

31 Read Shakespeare.

32 Hula hoop.

33 Have a Beatles night. Watch *A Hard Day's Night*, have British food and beer, and recite the lyrics to as many songs as you can remember.

34 Join Weight Watchers.

35 Figure out what Guinness record you'd like to break.

36 Give each other foot massages.

37 Try archery.

38 Rent a horror flick.

39 Find things to do for free.

40 Rent all the *I Love Lucy* episodes and recite the lines.

41 Hire a local chef to cook a meal at home.

42 Pretend you're living in the 1800s. No lights, power, or cars.

43 Crash a hotel Jacuzzi.

44 Sneak wine coolers into the movies.

45 Buy toys you played with as a kid: bubbles, silly putty, slinky, yo-yos.

46 Go plane watching at a local airport. Pack a six pack.

47 Walk in the rain drinking piña coladas

48 Make the largest, most fattening sundae you can.

49 Prepare a feast and deliver it to the homeless.

50 Wash each other's hair.

GREAT DATE MOVIES TO RENT

These films have nothing in common with each other. They range from current to classics. However, they appeal to all ages and all types of people. They are romantic and sexy—and not just chick flicks.

Have refreshments ready to enhance the experience:

- Chocolate
- Fruit
- Wine
- Tea
- Pastries

Stay away from salty foods, or things that will sit in your mouth, like peanut butter. Unless you're really into each other, mutually, in which case you can bring out the whipped cream.

1 *Casablanca*

2 *Ghost*

3 *Pretty Woman*

4 *Sabrina* (both versions)

5 *L.A. Story*

6 *Benny and Joon*

7 *The Big Easy*

8 *Bull Durham*

9 *Sleepless in Seattle*

10 *Love Is a Many Splendored Thing*

11 *Roman Holiday*

12 *While You Were Sleeping*

13 *Four Weddings and a Funeral*

14 *Notting Hill*

15 *When Harry Met Sally*

16 *Breakfast at Tiffany's*

17 *The Bodyguard*

18 *Say Anything*

19 *Romeo and Juliet (1997)*

20 *Titanic*

21 *An Officer and a Gentleman*

22 *Dirty Dancing*

23 *West Side Story*

24 *Bye Bye Birdie*

25 *Love, Actually*

26 *Arthur*

27 *The Maltese Falcon*

28 *The In-Laws*

29 *Shrek*

30 *Legally Blonde*

SIGNS THAT THINGS ARE GOING WELL

- You both are really having a great time.
- The other person tells you he or she would love to see you again.
- You can be yourself with this person.
- You feel good about yourself when the date ends.
- You commit to a second date.
- You can't stop thinking about each other until the second date.
- You spend more time on the phone planning your next date.
- You lose five pounds in three days.

FACTS ABOUT MEN AND WOMEN THAT WILL NEVER CHANGE

No matter how the battle of sexes evolves, there are things that just won't change. If you go into dating knowing these facts, you'll have a better sense of what men and women want.

For Women

It's all visual. Men are excited by a woman's external beauty first, not her brain. Brains come much later in the game. Women who believe otherwise will lose at the dating game because it's something they can't change. Women who hide their sex appeal in rebellion or to prove a point will have a much harder time finding a man. Real men *need the visual stimulation first.*

My advice to women: Glamour yourself up, look sexy, and I know you will truly love all the attention you will start getting.

Men and fat women. Most men don't like fat women. This may sound harsh and mean, and I'm sure I'll get lots of letters from fat people. That's why I use the word "most" to cover myself. I'm not making this up. It's what hundreds of men from all walks of life have told me.

However, most men don't like the "anorexic" look either. They love a woman who has curves in all the right places. So the good news is you don't have to be stick thin, but flab popping out of your midriff won't work either.

Clothing is crucial in how to accentuate your best qualities. If you got a beautiful back, wear a low V-cut outfit. Men like skin as long as it looks good.

My advice to women: Lose some weight. Get your body to a place that makes you look sexy. Re-vamp your wardrobe with outfits that highlight your best features. Spend that extra fifteen minutes exercising, or preparing yourself. You'll know when you've done this correctly. The phone will start ringing and you'll love it.

For Men

Men who don't have any money. Women hate this. Men who have no money are perceived to be lost, weak, lazy, and a misfit. Women have it hard enough making their own money and managing their own affairs in a male-dominated business world. It emasculates a man who either doesn't have a job, direction, or fat trust account.

My advice to men: Don't talk about your financial status right away. Try to get your life together if you want to attract a decent woman. Don't look at women as gold diggers (although they are out there), but even the most sincere woman doesn't want a freeloader, unless he has other redeeming qualities, like volunteering for the terminally ill, going for a great degree in something that has the potential of bringing in money, or taking care of all the household chores. It's a stretch, but it does happen.

Men who push sex before the woman is ready. Women hate being pushed into having sex without an "emotional" connection. Yes, women can be fickle. They might toss aside morals, values, and a game plan if they get drunk enough and the man is rich enough. But she'll hate herself the next morning. In an average situation, women still like to feel an emotional attachment before jumping in the sack.

My advice to men: If you want to score with a woman, show that you care about her, listen to her, and build her up. Don't mention sex. She doesn't need to hear the words. Subtle touches and setting the right mood are enough. Just be clear that women you have sex with will have an emotional feeling towards you, or they wouldn't have gone to bed with you, so be prepared to deal with it.

chapter ten:

Getting to Know Each Other— What to Say

One of the reasons dates turn out to be a disaster is because people get nervous and say all the wrong things.

There are stages in getting to know someone. It's very uncomfortable if, in the first few minutes you meet someone, he or she asks you how many lovers you have had. Or, "How do you feel about sex on the first date?" Or, "How much money do you make?" These are all areas that put people on the spot, and turn them off.

When first meeting someone, there are social tactics that need to be used that lead to the answers you really want to know. It's all about how to gain the other person's comfort in confiding in you. That is why we have small talk. Successful small talk leads to the meatier issues.

Beginning the Date

1 Give a compliment. Don't gush or go overboard. A nice "you look great" works.

2 Greet with a gift. Something small here, like a flower or a piece of chocolate.

3 Greet with a light hug hello.

4 Say you've been looking forward to this date

5 (For men) "Here, let me get that for you." Chivalry is very important on a date. It's what a gentleman should do and a woman *should let the man do*. It makes a man feel good about being in charge, being in control, and taking care of the woman. No matter how self-sufficient she is at work or home, on a date, the man needs to be the strong one. It's just the way it is.

6 (For women) "Thank you." Women need to let the man do all the gentlemanly things he can do. It shows he cares and wants to do the right thing. Don't be a bitch and take that away from him.

Women also need to lean over and open the lock for the man. Men hate it when she sits there like a stone-faced prude and won't show courtesy and lean over. The way you get into the car can really set the tone for the date.

How much chivalry is needed?

Do all the little things for each other that you heard about during the '50s. That's what romance is about. Men need to act like they are in charge, and women have to make them believe it.

The fear women have of this concept is that it will them back fifty years and makes them look like the meek, dependent souls their grandmothers were. Not! Not if you play it right. The romantic gestures work on a date. That's why you leave your work at the office, and turn up the charm romantically. It's a turn-on for men, and you'll get it back in many other ways.

SMALL TALK IN THE CAR

To avoid uncomfortable silent moments in the car, here are some suggestions to get you through. Remember, keep everything light. That's why it's called "small talk." You don't want any political shouting matches before you hit the first red light.

1. Discuss where you're going and the rest of the plans for the date.

2. Reminisce about how you met.

3. Talk about music. Look for some great music to put on.

4. Talk about driving. Any tickets? Ever been to traffic school?

5. Talk about what you did today, but keep it light and don't get into heavy areas.

6 Bring up some of your favorite TV shows and see if you can remember the lyrics to their theme songs.

7 Talk about your upcoming week. Just don't mention scary things, like taking your mom to get that lump checked. It will bring the mood down. Be positive.

8 Talk about how you prepared for the date, if there is a story to it.

9 Play the geography game, or animal or favorite food game (where you mention something in that category, and you have to take the last letter of that word to begin the next item).

10 Talk about your travels, and where you've been in life.

CONVERSATIONAL DOs AND DON'Ts

Here are some basics on how to have a great date, from the very beginning. Ignoring these points has contributed to some people not making it to their destination at all.

DOs

1 Do mention how you enjoyed talking to this person on the phone.

② Do ask positive questions.

③ Women—do be sexy, show a little leg, lean over and show some cleavage. Men—compliment her.

④ Do let the other person finish thoughts.

⑤ Do smile when you speak.

DON'Ts

① Don't ask about exes.

② Don't ask how many times he or she dates in a week.

③ Don't be a backseat driver.

④ Don't talk about marriage.

⑤ Don't talk on your cell phone, unless it's an emergency, or you need directions.

100 GETTING-TO-KNOW-YOU QUESTIONS

Here are some wise, thought-provoking, inquisitive things you can ask that will take away all those awkward, dead-silent moments, and at the same time see how much you really do have in common.

Once again, keep your answers light. These questions are not intended to really open you up, but rather to keep the conversation going.

People really *don't want to hear everything*, just enough to keep them guessing. It's a version of speed dating, but on a real date. Instead of twenty questions, it's 100 questions.

1. If you could change places with one person for a day, who would that be?

2. If you could change identities with one person for life, who would that be?

3. Do you have any superstitions?

4. If you had to leave your house in an emergency, never to return, and could only take one thing, what would that be?

5. If you could be a leader somewhere, either of a country or corporation, what would it be?

6. Can you go *anywhere* alone (a social event, trip, bar)?

7. If you could be one cartoon character, who would that be?

8 What decade would you like to have been born in?

9 If you could make a list of five people to get rid of and not get caught, who would they be?

10 If you could rob a casino, like the team in *Ocean's Eleven*, where no one really gets hurt, but you could get your family out of poverty—would you?

11 Could you sneak into anything without paying? A concert, a play, or seminar?

12 If you ate in a restaurant and the food and service were terrible, the worst you had ever experienced, could you sneak out without paying?

13 When you sleep, do you sleep on one side of the bed, or in the middle?

14 What was the most frightening horror movie you ever saw?

15 Did the movie *Jaws* make you afraid to go in the water?

16 Do you have an idol that you look up to?

17 When you were a kid, what TV show did you watch all the time?

18 If you were to go to a costume party, how would you dress?

19 If there were one food you could eat for a week, what would that be?

20 What are some of your most embarrassing moments?

21 Have you ever been really lucky? When was that?

22 Have you ever won a contest or lottery?

23 If you could spend a million dollars in one week, what would you spend it on?

24 Have you ever cheated on a test?

25 If you could be one of the characters from *The Wizard of Oz*, who would you be?

26 If you could write the story of your life from this moment on, how would it go?

27 Who are your dream people to invite over for dinner, from anywhere, from any era?

28 What book that you read as a kid affected you the most?

29 What talent do you wish you had been born with?

30 What would you like to go back in time to finish that is yet to be finished (like learning how to play an instrument, dance, etc.)?

31 What party did you have the best time at? What about the worst time?

32 What would I find on your nightstand right now?

33 What magazines would I find in your bathroom?

34 How do you unwind or pamper yourself?

35 What's your favorite time of year?

36 Who's on your Christmas list?

37 Did you save anything special from your childhood?

38 Did your mother ever throw out anything of yours that is now worth millions?

39 Have you ever answered a dating ad?

40 Of all the Baskin-Robbins flavors, what's your favorite?

41 What car describes you the best?

42 Have you ever been stuck in an elevator?

43 Have you ever saved anyone's life?

44 What's the best present you ever got?

45 Have you ever re-wrapped something from your house and given it to someone as a present?

46 Do you have any collections?

47 Have you ever fixed anyone up on a date?

48 If you could watch one Disney movie over and over again, what would it be?

49 What do you remember the best from your childhood neighborhood?

50 What's the best piece of advice a stranger ever gave you?

51 If you got up in the middle of the night to raid your fridge, what would you eat?

52 What's the oddest food you've ever tried? (Frogs legs?)

53 If you could play Santa Claus for one day, whose lives would you brighten up first?

54 What part of your place do you spend the most time in?

55 What kind of money would it take for you to pose in the nude?

56 How much money would it take for you to shave your head?

57 What's the worst trouble you ever got into?

58 What adult in your family do you have the most admiration for?

59 Do you have a best friend?

60 Is there anyone in your life that you want to say "I'm sorry" to?

61 Were you popular in high school? How would your high school friends describe you?

62 What's the longest time you ever went without bathing?

63 What's the most money you've spent on yourself?

64 If you had one day to spend without making any plans, what would you do?

65 If you could fly somewhere for one day where would you go?

66 Are you a picky eater? When you order a Subway sandwich, what do you get?

67 What's the biggest tip you ever left?

68 If you were only staying one night in a motel, would you leave a tip in the room?

69 What do you wear when you sleep?

70 Do you ever play pranks on anyone? What do you do?

71 What concert do you want to see so badly you'd pay almost any price for it?

72 What's your favorite cereal?

73 Is there anyone you're holding a grudge against? Why?

74 If you could be ruler of the planet, and declare one day of fun, what things would you do?

75 If I opened your closet right now, what would I see?

76 When you go to a person's home, do you snoop in the medicine cabinet?

77 Have you ever walked in on your parents having sex?

78 If I were to read your diary tomorrow, what do you think it would say?

79 Have you ever been a contestant on a TV game show?

80 Do you know how to program your VCR?

81 If you had to write your epitaph, what would it be?

82 Where do you see yourself in five years?

83 How do you spend a typical Sunday?

84 What's your main claim to fame?

85 If you could be any age again, what would that be?

86 What is the riskiest thing you ever did?

87 Would you rather enjoy a picnic in the country near a river, or spend it in the city in a 5-star restaurant?

88 Would you rather go on a submarine or a spaceship?

89 Have you ever had a life-changing experience?

90 What's your favorite outdoor activity? Indoor?

91 What movie have you seen most recently?

92 If I were to play back your messages, whom would they be from?

93 What lie did you tell your parents that you're still holding on to?

94 What music do you hate, but will tolerate if your date loves it?

95 Have you ever mooned anyone?

96 What's the wackiest thing you would do to get accepted into a club?

97 What offbeat thing will you put up with from the opposite sex: an annoying laugh, embarrassing dancing, or very picky eating?

98 What's the thing you used to fight your parents on as a kid and now you realize they were right?

99 What do you like most about yourself?

100 What's been your favorite question so far?

50 *Sexy* Getting-To-Know-You Questions

Now that you're getting to know each other, here's a riskier, sexier list.

1 What part of your body is the easiest to arouse?

2 What would you settle for...great sex? Or a great love?

3 Would you ever play strip poker with a bunch of strangers? How far would you go?

4 For $100, would you strip for your date? $1,000? $10,000?

5 Would you fake an orgasm just to avoid hurting your lover's feelings?

6 How many lovers have you looked back at and wondered, "what the hell was I thinking?"

7 Do you believe in sex on a first date?

8 Have you ever used aphrodisiacs to get aroused? What did you use?

9 Have you ever watched a porn flick to get aroused?

10 Have you ever made your own personal adult video?

11 If your partner cheated on you, would you want to know?

12 Define "lust" and "love."

13 Have you ever done anything sexual that you are now sorry for?

14 Have you ever tried a different position that physically hurt you?

15 Have you ever role-played? Like dressing up as a cop and arresting your lover?

16 What's the kinkiest thing you've done? Threesomes? Orgies? Swapping?

17 What's your wildest sexual fantasy?

18 Have you ever had sex in a public place? Under a bridge? At the park? In the back of a restaurant?

19 When you wake up with your lover in the morning what would you prefer...taking a shower together, or sharing a cup of cocoa?

20 Where's the sexiest place to go to get romantic with you?

21 Are you a member of the "mile high club"?

22 Do you remember your first time? What was that like?

23 If someone were to describe that one unique thing you like to do during sex, what would it be?

24 Where's the smallest place you ever did it?

25 Have your parents ever walked in on you?

26 When you get comfortable with your lover, do you close the bathroom door?

27 What gets you aroused more, looking at a sexy magazine or a porn flick?

28 Have you ever had sex with a lover even after you broke up?

29 What's the thing that turns you on most about the opposite sex, looks, money, or the car they drive?

30 What's the longest time you've spent having sex?

31 Have you ever gone on vacation with someone and never left the room?

32 Would you rather your lover have a great body but an ugly face, or not such a great body and a gorgeous face?

33 What's your best "getting caught" story?

34 When you're home alone, what do you wear?

35 What's the sexiest thing you've done in public (swim in the nude, go topless on a beach, have sex at someone else's wedding)?

36 What's the longest time you've gone without having sex?

37 Have you ever destroyed any property during sex?

38 Do you consider cyber sex cheating?

39 Would you be jealous if your lover became friends with an ex-love?

40 Would you have sex to get the job?

41 Would you participate in an indecent proposal, where for a $100,000 you would have sex with someone, while committed to someone else? Would it matter if you were married?

42 Write a sexy poem.

43 If you were on a no-carbs diet, and your lover asked you lick chocolate off of him or her, would you go off your diet?

44 How much would it affect your lovemaking if you were in a motel/hotel that had thin walls and squeaky beds?

45 How did you learn about sex?

46 What would you like to change about yourself in order to be a better lover?

47 Does size matter?

48 Who do you think make better lovers, young studs or older, more experienced people?

49 How do you feel when your lover undresses the wait-ress with his eyes in a restaurant? What about your girl flirting with the cute bartender?

50 Do you like sex?

I know how much you drink on the date will deter-mine how detailed you get with your answers to any of these questions. Please refrain from getting too detailed, as you don't want to regret anything you said later.

You also don't want to bring up negative things going on in your life. Remember, it's a date, *not a therapy session.*

These questions are intended to be:

a) A way to get to know the other person better.

b) A stepping stone to learning things that you may not normally learn on a first date.

c) A gauge of the ethics and values of your date to see how they match yours.

d) Ice breakers during silent awkward moments.

e) A way to have fun and laughs.

f) A way to see if you want a second date.

Tips to Not Turning Each Other Off

1 If people don't want to answer the questions, don't be pushy. Give people their space.

2 While these questions are intended for fun, hear the person out. You may not agree, but don't chew him or her out either. Even if he or she turns out to be an asshole, you never know whom he or she knows.

3 Maintain eye contact while he or she is talking to you, unless of course one of you is driving. If you're walking and talking, it's rude to walk a few blocks ahead of your date. It's a date, not speed walking (unless you really *are* speed walking).

4 If someone doesn't know something, don't make him or her feel like an idiot. Not everyone was fortunate enough to graduate from high school.

Use all this to your advantage to help you make the best impression you can.

You'll never get a second chance to make a good first impression.

chapter eleven

Sex...How Far Should You Go on the First Date?

What's the difference between *sex* and *sexual chemistry*?

Sex—is sex. It's all physical, with no emotional attachments. The man was horny, the woman was willing. End of story.

Sexual chemistry implies a deeper, more emotional connection. This still doesn't mean you'll get called back again, but there is an unexplainable initial attraction that feels like it might go somewhere.

Sexual chemistry can either blow up in your face really fast or continue to grow, depending on how much more you get to know this person you're with. So many times you hear how the date starts off great, great conversation, great "chemistry," only to find out later that this guy is a real jerk. Or that the woman is a whiner, complainer, and nag, and suddenly this beautiful woman reminds you of your sixth grade teacher, the one with the red marker.

So how do you know whether to have sex or not?

You can't possibly know. It's the first date, damn it. How do you really know anything about this person? The first date is a total façade. If it's not, it should be.

But this isn't helping you any, so here goes.

Ladies, you want to know: if you have sex on the first date, are you a big fat slut?

(Men, you don't worry if you have sex on the first date. For most of you, you'll still be able to chug back some beers with your friends, while "what's her name" is crying by the phone.)

So, ladies, the answer to whether having sex on a first date is okay is simple.

Yes.

It's okay to have sex on a first date—if you take a second to think about the consequences.

Here's what you should ask yourself:

▪ How will I feel if I never see this person again?
▪ Am I putting myself in harm's way?

If you go into it knowing that there's a good, well actually a *great*, chance nothing will come of this, and you are using all the protection humanly possible, and you feel you're not with some psychopath, then why not?

(I know this goes without saying, but I'm going to say it anyway. *Always have safe sex.* There's nothing wrong with packing a condom (or two) in your slinky little evening bag—if he's prepared you won't need it, but if he's not, you can take charge and make sure you don't get carried away. If he refuses to use a rubber for any reason, *run*, and I do mean *RUN*. In today's world, you can't afford to take this chance.)

Who am I to judge what you do? Just be sure you can handle the aftermath, such as:

- After sex there's a chance he'll leave or kick you out.
- He may never call again.
- He may become obsessed with you.
- He could be a real nut.
- He could have some sort of rash or other communicable disease that he didn't disclose to you.

The Sex Barometer—To Have Sex or Not to Have?

During the whole date, both of you have this sex barometer going up and down in your head.

For Men

1. When you first lay eyes on each other, and there's an attraction—the sex barometer goes up.

2. Then she tells you how to drive—barometer goes down.

3. Then she lays her hand on your knee—barometer goes up.

4. Then she orders the most expensive thing on the menu, and you have no money left for the tip and drinks afterwards—barometer goes down.

5. Then she offers to pay for the drinks afterwards—barometer goes up.

6 During drinks she tells you she's still in love with her ex—barometer goes down.

7 You then both get plastered—barometer is out the window.

For Ladies

1 He picks you up and is really cute—barometer goes up.

2 He cracks his knuckles all through the car ride—barometer goes down.

3 He compliments you and tells you how beautiful you are—barometer goes up (you can now live with the annoying sounds of loud cracking knuckles).

4 You get to the theatre and discover he's lost the tickets to a play you've been so excited to see—barometer goes down (you're wondering what kind of a dork he is).

5 He offers to pay double for whatever tickets he finds from a scalper, and pulls out a wad of cash—barometer goes up (you're thinking he's a problem solving kind of guy).

6 He falls asleep and snores during the whole play—barometer goes down (and you're totally embarrassed).

7 To make up for sleeping during the play because he was up all night studying for the bar exam, he takes you to his luxury condo, you guys get plastered—Once again, barometer out the window.

There are no dating rules about having or not having sex on a first date. Who am I, or anyone else, to tell another person what is right or wrong about it? It's like believing in a religion. It's very personal and private.

The only thing that I can tell you is that there are consequences for some. Some can handle them better than others. Some women love the power of making that decision, and walking away from it. *Know the kind of person you are.*

Can you handle having sex on the first date, knowing very little about the other person? Where he's been? What she is hiding? What the other person thinks or feels about you? If these are answers you don't care about, then you're the type that can handle having sex on the first date. But if you're the type who needs to know more about the other person, then you may want to hold back. You may not be the type to handle the pending aftermath.

Out of the hundreds of people I interviewed, most women hated themselves afterwards. They felt cheap, used, and stupid. There were a handful of women who succeeded with sex on the first date, but it's rare. If you have the type of personality that is willing to take the risk, and not jump out of fast-moving train afterwards, then you could be one of these people who truly does find a soul mate after sex on a first date.

I hate statistics. I'm talking about statistics in the dating world. The only number I used in the whole book is how many singles are really out there. This is based on a scientific compilation by the Census Bureau. There is one statistic used constantly in the dating world that I don't buy. That's "How many people marry the person they had sex with on the first date?" Answer: very few. As little as 2 percent. The reason I hate this study is because it really can't be proven. It's impossible to gather all the data and make sense of it. Remember one thing: I can guarantee you that the people who didn't marry the person they had sex with on the first date wouldn't have anyway, regardless of whether or not they had sex.

Having sex on the first date does not ruin your chances for marrying that person afterwards. Either you're meant to be together or not. Sex has nothing to do with that. The good thing about having sex on the first date is it makes you realize if you want to see this person again, without having to go out on countless dates. You'll see at the beginning if you click sexually. The bad thing is that you're sleeping with a stranger.

chapter twelve:

The Second Date

The second date should be a continuation of the first date, where the fun factor should still be strong. This is still too early to want a commitment or to start driving through neighborhoods pointing out what house you want to buy. You may scare your date off.

Even if you've already had sex, it's never too late to talk about what you really like about it. You may find out that you both share the same fantasy of dressing up like little red riding hood and the big bad wolf and running through the forest to grandma's, only to find out you never make it to grandma's.

Here's What the Second Date Should Tell You

1 It shows there's potential and a mutual interest.

2 It reveals more about that person, because they are more comfortable with you and you can see if the compatibility factor is still there.

3 You can see if the sexual chemistry is real, or if it was the late nightcap that made this person better looking.

202 ■ dating confidential

4 Nasty habits can start creeping in, such as talking on the cell in front you, belching, knuckle-cracking during a movie, teeth grinding, and nail biting.

5 You'll see if you want a third date.

The third date is where the heavier issues really start creeping in, such as goals in life, what your family is really like, past relationships, political views, and sexual desires.

Five Major Things You Need to Reveal at the End of the First Date, While Planning the Second

1 Your real job

2 Your real name

3 Your real sex

4 Your real parental status

5 Your real intentions about staying in town (did you just apply for your dream job in Asia?)

FAQs about the Second Date

Here is a list of the most common concerns about the second date.

1 Q: You've hidden your real self on the first date, how much do you reveal now?

A: Just a little more. Still don't talk about how your biological clock is ticking and you want a baby now! You should reveal, however, if you never want to get married nor have kids. That way you're not misleading anyone.

2 Q: What should you do when you find out that your date is still hung up on an ex?

A: Be a good listener. Let him or her get the past off his or her chest for a few minutes. However, if this hang up totally dominates the date, then cut the date short, politely. You don't mind being a good friend, but you're not a therapist. Then let him or her call you when he or she is ready. If you put any pressure on someone who is still emotionally hung up on someone else, then you'll never get a true sense if he or she is just dating you from loneliness. Take a few steps back to see if he or she comes forward.

3 Q: What do you do when you find out your date totally lied about what he or she does for a living? That he or she really isn't an attorney, but a paralegal?

A: If he or she blatantly said he or she was a lawyer, and not in the "legal profession," then you don't want to date a blatant liar. There's a big difference between not revealing everything there is to know about yourself, or being vague, versus an outright lie. That would really piss me off.

4 **Q:** When do I tell him I have four kids under the age of three?

A: You should have said that on the phone call before the first date starts. Information like this is crucial. What you don't want to do is tell someone how you have four screaming brats who are holding you back from meeting men. A simple, "I have four kids" on the initial call will gently let that person know a very important piece of information about you.

5 **Q:** What if I find out there's a really weird kinky side to this person?

A: This is where all the red flags really start popping up. Kinky as in, liking to wear a diaper and pretending to be a baby, is much deeper and is masking a thousand other things. Unless you like playing "mommy," I'd run.

6 **Q:** Is it too early to invite my date over to my place and cook him dinner?

A: There are no hard rules for this. Anyone who says it's too early couldn't possibly be coming from any place of really knowing what's going on. That's because things spark and develop for people at different times.

When it feels right, you'll know it because you both can't stop thinking about each other since the first date, and have no interest in dating other people, at least for now.

7 Q: Is it necessary to tell my date I'm considering moving out of state?

A: Yes. This way you won't be blamed for breaking someone's heart. You can decide together how far you want to take this.

8 Q: Can I take my date to a family function?

A: Yes. Just remember that your date will judge you by your family. If you're Marilyn Munster, then you may want to consider waiting before introducing your date to Uncle Herman.

9 Q: If I had sex on the first date, am I obligated to have it again on the second?

A: No. You should never feel obligated to have sex, even when you're married. It should be mutual, consensual, and something you both want. If you feel pressured in any way, then you should consider cutting the date short. You don't want the potential relationship to be only based on sex. When that wears down, you may find yourself holding lots of broken condoms and a broken heart.

10 **Q:** What if I find out this person is truly threatened by the fact that I make so much more money than he does?

A: This can be a red flag because it shows his insecurity. He may feel guilty if it turns out you have the means to pay for more elaborate dates. This type of man is tricky because men have been taught that they have to make more money than the woman. Whatever you do, don't go to really expensive places because that will make him feel "less than a man." A man judges his worth by two things: the size of his penis and the size of his wallet.

Continue having the fun thing going on the second date and by the end of it you should be able to figure out if this person is worth going out with. If he's too extreme, and keeps rubbing your income in your face, then he has deeper issues and I'd dump him right away. If it's just that he doesn't want to feel like a free-loader, then it sounds like he's just being a nice guy and he's probably worth getting to know better.

You need to find out why he's threatened and how he handles it. If he's threatened because he thinks you will look down on him, then you need to show him you're okay with it, as long as you truly are. If you sincerely are bugged by the fact that you make more money, then you shouldn't be dating him. Just remember that it's normal for him to feel threatened, but if he's too "bitchy" about it, then it's not worth it.

11 Q: On the second date I had the chance to meet her mother. She's three hundred pounds and lives off her ex-husband. Will my date turn out just like her mother? A: No. Although it's been said that you judge a girl by the way her mother looks, there really is no believable data that supports this. If anything, girls who have obese moms work hard at not being like that.

We don't know the circumstances that cause these women to blow up. Yes it's true that there is a link between genetics and obesity, but it doesn't mean your date has inherited this gene. Don't ever allow generalities, gossip, and projected fear to stand in your way. It's a cop out, wimpy, and spineless. Unless you see your date exhibiting other bizarre habits, like bingeing and purging, her fat, unemployed mother is not who you're dating.

IN CONCLUSION

I know how scary the dating world is. It's filled with so many expectations and unknowns.

This book is your book. It's filled with useful tips that have been given to me by singles from all walks of life. Consider me the messenger. The messenger of information. The messenger of hope. The messenger of faith.

And although I've held this information captive for many years thinking there were already too many dating books out there, it's no longer necessary for me to keep my knowledge to myself.

There are people who do need to know what's what. What's the truth and what's fiction. My knowledge is no longer confidential. That would be selfish of me. I'm happy I've been able to share *Dating Confidential* with you and hopefully make your love life a little less traumatic and confusing.

Here Is What I Want You to Walk Away With:

1. Your soul mate really is out there.

2. Don't beat yourself up if you feel like you messed up on the first date. If it's truly meant to be, it will happen.

3. If you're on a really lousy date, don't make a big deal out of it. Try to end it on a good note and you can cut the date short. This too shall pass.

4. The other person is just as nervous as you are.

5. Don't waste time with a person who is really not into you. With millions of singles out there you truly do you have your pick.

Follow these tips. They do work. I know it because they câme from daters like you. Whenever you feel in doubt, at a loss for words, or insecure about what's going on, turn to *Dating Confidential*. Share it with your friends.

You can be their sounding board, because *you* now know what's *really* going on.

About the Author

Hedda Muskat, formerly a producer and writer on television's longest running dating show, *Love Connection*, is co-author of *Dating: A Single's Guide to a Fun, Flirtatious, and Possibly Meaningful Social Life*.

Hedda is the Human Interest Producer on the hit show, *The Ellen DeGeneres Show*. She was previously a producer on *The Montel Williams Show, Howie Mandel* and *Martin Short*. She holds a BA in Communications from Ryerson University, Toronto, Canada. Hedda is also the author of a successful book from the '80s, *The Yuppie Cookbook*. She resides in Los Angeles, California with her husband and daughter.